Tales Along
Lake Tahoe Shores
A Sentimental Journey

by
David & Gayle Woodruff

El Camino Sierra Publishing
elcaminosierra395@gmail.com
1326 Kimmerling Rd # A
Gardnerville, NV 89460

ISBN-979-8-218-13560-7

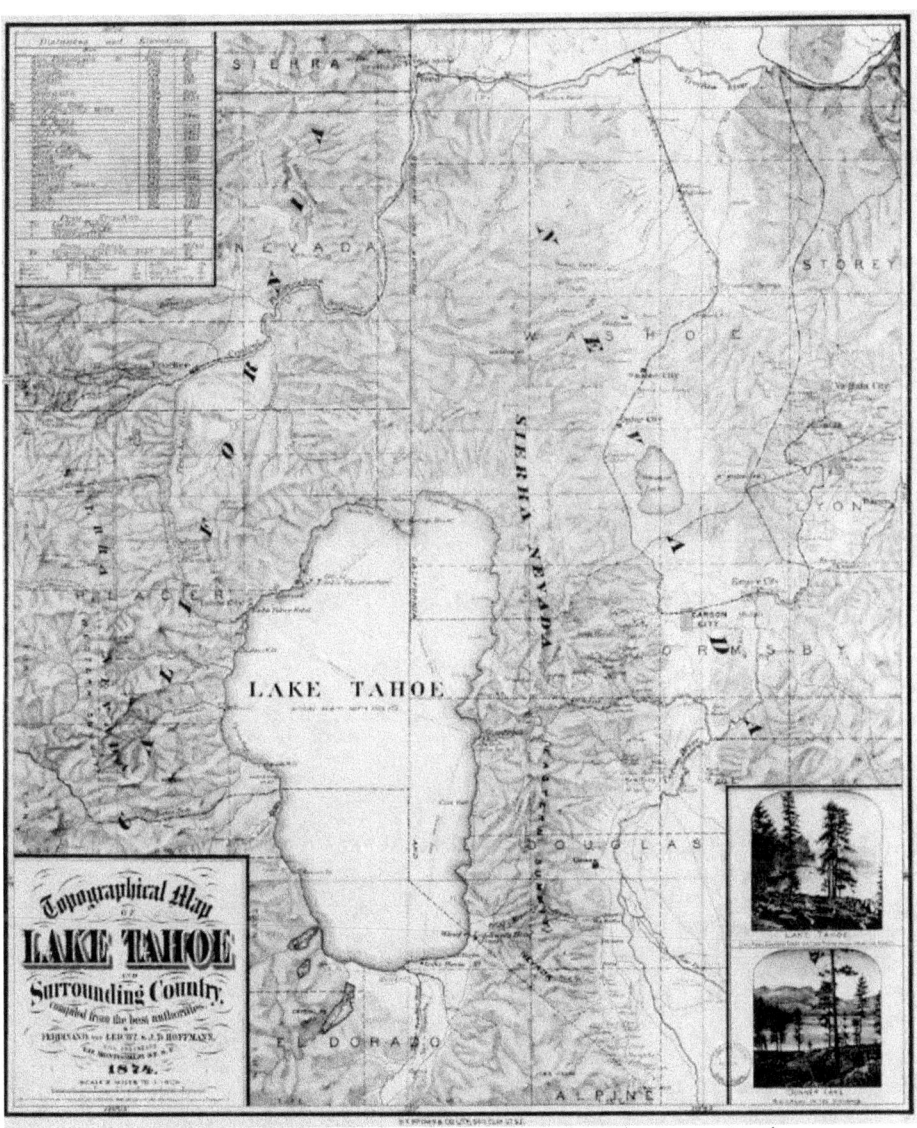

One of the first accurate maps of the Lake Tahoe area- 1874.

CONTENTS

CONTENTS

Guests coming and going on the pier at Brockway Hot Springs Resort on Lake Tahoe's north shore, with the *S.S. Tahoe* in the background.

ACKNOWLEDGMENTS

There are always so many people that are involved in projects such as this that one becomes fearful important contributors will inadvertently be overlooked in the acknowledgments. That said, there is absolutely no way we could have accomplished this passion of ours without the assistance of our many dear relatives, friends, acquaintances, and supporters.

Thank you to our dear friends and "editors extraordinaire" Kerry Roeser and Marye Roeser for the hours spent tediously editing these many pages of text. We are very, very grateful to Kerry and Marye for their help...and their friendship. This book could not have been completed without their invaluable assistance. And we express our sincere appreciation to Mike Elam, for providing an additional set of eyes for the editing process.

We extend a very large amount of gratitude to the Lake Tahoe Historical Society at South Lake Tahoe, specifically Paula Peterson, Board President, and Diane Johnson, Museum Curator. Their passion, along with the other LTHS Board members, for keeping the history of the Lake Tahoe area relevant, is an inspiration for all who enjoy local and regional history, and has been instrumental in our research.

There are many historians and scholars who have done extensive and very detailed research on the history of our beloved Lake Tahoe, and whose work we have utilized considerably in putting together our own narrative of this magnificent lake's history. First and foremost is Edward B. Scott. His two volume *The Saga of Lake Tahoe* is "the" authority on Lake Tahoe history. The byline on his title page states, "A complete documentation of Lake Tahoe's development over the last one-hundred years." We could not agree more. Tahoe resident Mark McLaughlin has written numerous books on Lake Tahoe and California history. He also writes history columns for newspapers and magazines, and is a lecturer on a variety of Lake Tahoe topics. There is no one that we know of that is more knowledgeable on all matters Lake Tahoe. Scholars and authors, Gary Noy and Scott Lankford, have both researched and written extensively on the "Lake," and we have enjoyed their books and writing immensely. And there are many, many more who have probed and scrutinized the history of Lake Tahoe...and we give thanks to you all.

Our sincere appreciation extends to all the delightful organizations, who work so hard, often with the efforts of only volunteers, keeping the story of our collective heritage available for learning and research. Among the many important institutions are: North Lake Tahoe Historical Society, Truckee-Donner Historical Society, Alpine County Historical Society, Douglas County Historical Society, Nevada Historical Society, the University of Nevada Online Digital Collections, the Western Nevada Historic Photo Collection, and many, many more.

It would not be fitting, if we did not acknowledge the influence of David's father on us becoming authors. Harry C. Woodruff researched, composed, and produced several technical guides relating to shortwave and microwave (electromagnetic wave- not microwave ovens), along with books on chemistry and astronomy for adolescents. He was also a technical writer at his aerospace job. We are humbled to be able to "follow in his footsteps."

And lastly, the positive feedback we have received from the hundreds of people who have not only expressed enjoyment of the first three books in our "Tales Along" series, but who have also encouraged us to pen another book. All of this has provided us the inspiration and motivation for this fourth book on Eastern Sierra history. Thank you!

Time at Lake Tahoe is time well spent- 1915.

INTRODUCTION

The Lake Tahoe region has long been a place that holds a sentimental and romantic attraction to most of the people who visit, as well as to those who are fortunate enough to live there. This certainly has been true for the two of us.

Perhaps nowhere else does scenery so sublime present itself so magnificently and on such a grand scale as it does while viewing this alpine mountain gem. The deep forests, soaring peaks, and shimmering sapphire waters combine to make a landscape so beautiful that one sometimes thinks only the innovators and creators from a Hollywood movie studio could create a scene so perfect. A visit to this enchanted land becomes the basis of what dreams are made of.

We both clearly remember our own special sentiments of what author Mark Twain referred to as "the fairest picture the whole world affords." Having met there as youngins' in 1976 (Gayle while cashiering at Raley's and David as the Hostess Cake sales-rep), Lake Tahoe has always held a special place in our hearts and minds. And even while living in some of the most enchanted lands on earth (Death Valley, Mono Lake, and the Owens Valley), the allure of Lake Tahoe was never far away for us.

Over time, it became very clear that we were not alone in holding Lake Tahoe in such sentimental and romantic regard. With near unanimity, our Eastern Sierra neighbors, our out-of-area friends and relatives, and visitors we would meet at work or on the trail - all seemed to share that same starry-eyed wonderment of "that lake" that had created so many special and enduring memories for them.

We listened to hundreds of people share their heartfelt reminiscence of their own personal Lake Tahoe experiences. Many expressed their feelings in moving and often emotional reflection. It was clear this iconic region has led to the creation of lifelong remembrances with nearly all who have visited it.

We began to think of those from the generations before us who have lived, traveled, and vacationed in the Lake Tahoe area. What were their stories? Were emotional ties to it as strong then as they are today?

Humankind has been enjoying the beauty and magical qualities of Lake Tahoe for millenniums. Ancestors of the Washo and Paiute peoples have savored its spellbinding enchantment for thousands of years. We can only imagine the sense of well being and contentment these First Peoples enjoyed at this very special place.

Euro settlers "discovered" Lake Tahoe and its allurement by the mid 19th century. Very quickly, in the words of John Muir, "Thousands of tired, nerve-shaken, over-civilized people were {sic} beginning to find out that going to the mountains {and Lake Tahoe} is going home." Word of the rejuvenating and uplifting powers of a visit to Lake Tahoe spread far and wide, and humanity has been seeking out its mystical efficacy ever since.

In *Tales Along Lake Tahoe Shores*, we bring to you a variety of the many human stories of time well spent and dreams grown big at "Big Blue." We believe the tales are interesting, often amusing, and all of them entertaining. It is our hope that while our readers create their own special memories at this enchanted locale, they also reflect upon the many extraordinary life stories of those who have come before.

"I go to nature to be soothed, healed and have my senses put in order."
John Burroughs

Two young boys from the Washo Tribe, enjoying Lake Tahoe, as have their ancestors for thousands of years.

CHAPTER ONE

Da ow aga
"The Lake"

DIT' EH HU (THE TERRITORY)

*"The Maker of All Things was counting out seeds that were
to become the different tribes. He counted them out on a big
winnowing tray in equal numbers. West Wind, the mischievous
wind, watched until the Maker had divided the seeds into
equal piles on the basket. Then he blew a gust of wind that
scattered the seeds to east. Most of the seeds that were to have
been the Washo people were blown away. That is why the Washo
are fewer in number than other tribes."*
Washo legend- As retold by Jo Ann Nevers

Most visitors to Lake Tahoe know little to nothing about the people that
have inhabited this area for millenniums. The name Washoe (or Washo as
most of the tribal members prefer) is a corruption of the Native word Wa
She Shu (people from here). Anthropologists estimate that as many as 3,000
Washo lived in their ancestral homeland. Though the peripheral areas were
often shared with their neighbors the Paiute, Shoshone, Maidu, and Miwok,
Lake Tahoe was the center of the Washo universe.

The great diversity of climate, geography, and elevation within their
homeland provided the Washo a wide range of foods and materials essential
to life. Lake Tahoe provided bountiful fish and game for sustenance during
the warmer climes. The lower elevations of the Eagle, Washoe, and Carson
Valleys contained an abundant supply of piñon pine (nuts) and wild game,
and offered much milder winters.

The importance of the "spoken" word has been paramount to the culture
of most Native American tribes. History was passed down from generation
to generation by stories told by the elders. Dates and times were not deemed
as important as notions of place and homeland which helped establish a
sense of identity and belonging for Native American cultures. Because of
these differences from "euro-norms" in recording the past, Native American
history has often been overlooked or dismissed by mainstream academia, and very little of their history has been researched or published.

The Washo mostly gathered in three groups: the Wel mel ti, who lived in
the Truckee Meadows and north as far as Honey Lake, the Pau wa lu, who
inhabited around the Carson Valley and Pine Nut Mountains, and the Hung
a lei ti, who lived further south.

1

The three bands came together throughout the year for special events and gatherings. During the summer, each of the three regional groups would choose a different locale at Lake Tahoe as their center. There were often cross group marriages, or a person simply might choose to switch from one group to another. It was advantageous to continue living within the area where she or he grew up. Having an intimate knowledge of the land enabled one to find and harvest the foods and medicines needed. Familiarity with local game and their habits improved the success of one's hunting.

The Washo never hunted for "sport," and plants were never gathered unless they were going to be used. They keenly monitored their environment and never over harvested their resources. Special celebrations and prayer were offered before and after wild game were taken.

Washo legends tell of several creatures that had special powers and lived in their lands. Stories were told of "Water Babies," who inhabited various lakes (including Lake Tahoe), and were very powerful. It was said they sometimes would cause illness or death, but their presence could also be a good omen. Water Babies lived at Cave Rock, and would be visited by Washo healers to show respect and to renew their powers. A man-eating giant that preyed upon the neglectful and unmindful could also be found there.

In the middle of Lake Tahoe lived a giant man-eating creature, this one a bird. It was named Ong and was said to be so powerful, that trees would bend when he beat his wings. According to Washo legend, one day a Washo man was snatched up by Ong and taken to its nest. Fortunately, the man was not eaten right away because Ong had another person to eat. The Washo man watched the giant bird eat and noticed that it closed its eyes to chew. The man got an idea. Every time the bird closed its eyes he threw several arrows into its open mouth. By nightfall Ong was very sick. A storm raged through the night, and by morning the monster was dead. The Washo man plucked out one of Ong's massive feathers and used it as a boat to reach the shore. Some say that Ong's nest remains in Lake Tahoe's waters, submerged out of sight.

Spring, summer, and fall each provided their own valuable food resources. As soon as the snow had melted enough to allow access, the young adult Washos would begin making the trip to the shores of Da ow aga (Lake Tahoe). Soon, the majority of the tribe would make its way to the sacred lake for a large gathering. People would socialize, play a variety of games, and hold contests of skill.

Lake Tahoe provided an abundance of fish, and the Washo people were very adept at catching them. Some of the harvest was eaten fresh, and much was dried for later use. Fishing usually began in early June. There were so many fish that the Washo people would wade into the water and scoop them up with baskets. They would then toss the fish onto shore to be cleaned and placed on racks to dry. At the height of the fishing, the Washo continued into the night by torchlight. The fires created just enough light to reflect off the silvery back of the fish so the people could keep working.

The runs of fish lasted for about two weeks. Large fresh fish were wrapped in sunflower leaves and placed under the coals, and smaller fish were cooked in coarsely woven baskets with coals or hot rocks. Dried or smoked fish could be stored for several weeks. The process added flavor and kept insects away. Dried fish was eaten as a kind of jerky, boiled and rehydrated, and added to other foods as well.

The Lake Tahoe Basin also offered several types of berries, wild rhubarb, cat tail seeds, tiger lily seeds, sunflower seeds, wild onions, wild mustard, wild spinach, wild potatoes and sweet potatoes, tule root, wild turnips, wild celery, and countless other edible and medicinal plants. Many plants had a very short life cycle, and the Washo maintained very accurate information about the location and habits of these plants. The Washo understood the growth cycles of plants, the effects of weather on growth, and also had intimate knowledge of soils and specific growing conditions. This type of knowledge was passed from generation to generation through legends and story telling.

But winters, even in the lowlands of the valleys, were cold, often snowy, and very little food could be gathered. The Washo people ate mostly what they had stored from the other seasons. Pine nuts in particular were greatly prized. They were abundant, fairly easy to harvest, and could be stored for long periods once they were roasted. The prized nuts would also be pounded in to a fine flour, which could be made into a mush, soup or biscuit.

The Washo are known for weaving some of the most beautiful Native American baskets. Willow was the main material used. Some baskets were tightly woven and used for holding water. Looser woven baskets would be used for sifting seeds and nuts. Some baskets were specifically made for carrying babies.

The arrival of the Euro-Americans changed the Washo way of life in almost every way. In just a few years, trees were cut down, settlers' livestock harshly grazed the land, game was taken in great numbers, and the Lake Tahoe fishery was almost fished out. At the height, 70,000 pounds of fish were taken from the Lake in one season by these commercial fishermen.

Several Washo leaders emerged, speaking on behalf of their community. Some Euro-American settlers came to the Washo's defense. The transition from their traditional lives to the new life among the Euro-Americans was difficult. In 1917, some land was purchased and set aside for the Washo. Additional acreage was obtained over the next several decades. There are now five separate bands comprising the Washo Tribe: Carson, Stewart, Dresslerville, Woodfords, and Reno-Sparks. There are approximately 1,550 registered tribal members today.

Over the years the Washo have organized groups that promote traditional well being, respect, and generosity in the people including: the Washo Warrior Society, White Bison Society, Culture Camp, and tribal government groups like Project Venture.

As a way of further promoting Washo culture, the tribal government has enacted laws that allow special hunting and fishing privileges to people that are making and using traditional hunting and fishing devices.

We owe much to the Washo people and their ancestors. They were (and still are) excellent stewards of the land, and have done much to help Euro-Americans better understand the ways of living sustainably.

A family of Washo people at Lake Tahoe.

A Washo woman at her Lake Tahoe summer home.

CHAPTER TWO
"FLY ON IN"
Sky Harbor Casino

After World War Two, the American public was on the move. After four years of gas rationing, people were traveling, and many were finding their way to "Big Blue." The Lake Tahoe Railroad, which operated between Truckee and Tahoe City, had ceased operation in 1943, leaving Lake Tahoe accessible only by automobile.

Despite its growing popularity, Lake Tahoe had no airport for the first four decades of the 1900s. The Lake's high elevation and changeable weather created difficult conditions to land an airplane. But as technology increased and the demand for faster means of travel grew, entrepreneurs felt the time was right to offer air service to the Lake Tahoe Basin.

In 1946, businessmen Antone Gatto and E.W. Heple obtained several acres of land just northwest of where Kingsbury Grade meets U.S. Hwy. 50. The area today is known as Rabe Meadows, named after the Rabe family. They used to drive their cattle up Kingsbury Grade from the Carson Valley to graze in the meadows prior to the auto road being built.

A creek flowing through the property was relocated and a portion of the beautiful meadow filled in. Gatto and Heple's plan was to build a casino with an adjacent landing strip. They felt there were many high rollers who would jump at the chance to fly-in to their new gambling house. A small terminal was also built next to the dirt landing strip. The "airport" and casino were christened "Sky Harbor."

The casino featured big name entertainment, including the likes of the Nat Cole Trio. High rollers did indeed "fly-in," staying at Sky Harbor as well as other nearby Stateline, Nevada casinos.

But the landing strip was plagued with problems, including several plane crashes...some resulting in fatalities. Despite its 5,000-foot length, tall trees made visibility difficult, and the landing strip was considered too steep. High winds and a sharp descent added to the airport's challenges.

The airport was short lived, closing in 1950 due to safety concerns. Lake Tahoe was once again without an airport, until a runway was opened at the current South Tahoe airport site in 1958. The Sky Harbor Casino closed just a few years after the landing strip's closure.

In 1978, a casino developer bought the property and initiated plans to build a nine story casino, "Ted Jennings Palace." Foundations were even laid before the U.S. Forest Service stepped in, purchased the property, and work on the casino stopped.

Today, the former Sky Harbor location is one of the best natural areas near Stateline, NV, with several miles of scenic trails. The Lam Watah Nature Trail system offers visitors to Tahoe South a pleasant stroll along lush meadows, beaver ponds, a magnificent Jeffrey Pine Forest, and access to Nevada Beach.

The trailhead is located on Kahle Dr., just west of Hwy. 50, a bit north of its intersection with Kingsbury Grade.

Sky Harbor landing strip and casino, near Kingsbury Grade and Hwy. 50.

Sky Harbor Casino catered to the well heeled set who would fly in to the "dicey" adjacent landing strip to enjoy their Lake Tahoe gaming action.

CHAPTER THREE

PICNIC PAVILION
George Newhall's Skunk Harbor

Lake Tahoe enjoys a fair amount of lesser-known tales of history that can be found tucked away in its sheltered coves. On Tahoe's east shore, a little north of Glenbrook, nestled away in a dense forest of pine and incense cedar, and accessible only by a short, steep hike...sits one of the most magnificent estates to have graced Lake Tahoe's shores from its historic past. The impressive stone structure sits at the edge of secluded Skunk Harbor, and commands a breathtaking view of Lake Tahoe and the mountains around the west shore.

In the early 1920s, wealthy and socially prominent George Newhall bought a huge piece of lakefront property there. Newhall was the son of wealthy San Francisco area businessman Henry Mayo Newhall. Henry amassed a huge fortune during and after the California Gold Rush. His company, Newhall Land and Farming Company, owned property in both northern and southern California and, at its peak, totaled over 143,000 acres. The Southern California portion became known as the Newhall Ranch. The Southern Pacific Railroad named its station after him and so began the town of Newhall. Over time, the towns of Saugus, Santa Clarita, and Valencia were all carved out of Newhall's property.

Henry Newhall had five boys. Some went on to pursue their own business ventures, but youngest son George Newhall stayed on with the family's land company. As land was developed and sold, George became even wealthier. He built an opulent mansion in the exclusive community of Hillsborough above San Francisco, followed soon by a palatial summer home estate a few miles north of Emerald Bay. He named his summer home Rubicon Lodge.

For a wedding gift for his wife Caroline, Newhall purchased several miles of secluded waterfront known as Skunk Harbor on Lake Tahoe's east shore. George Newhall built what he referred to as a "picnic pavilion." The pavilion included a huge stone main house, outbuildings, boathouse, and a several hundred-foot-long dock. Everything had to be brought in by boat...at great expense. The estate became the setting for exclusive parties, featuring motorboats, elaborate banquets, sunbathing, and other activities and entertainments afforded by the opulent lifestyle of the very wealthy during the 1920s.

George Newhall passed away in 1929, and the parties at Skunk Harbor came to an end. A caretaker maintained the building and grounds, but wife Caroline and the rest of the family stopped coming to their Lake Tahoe "picnic pavilion."

George Newhall inherited his family's land and cattle company and was one of the wealthiest men on the west coast during the 1920s.

In the mid-1930s, wealthy George Whittell Jr. (see chapter twelve) acquired several thousand acres of the Lake Tahoe Basin, including the Newhall property. While building his own "Thunderbird Lodge" just a few miles north of the Skunk Harbor property, Whittell lived in Newhall's former "picnic pavilion" at Skunk Harbor. Once Thunderbird Lodge was completed, Whittell would occasionally use the former Newhall estate for guest accommodations.

George Whittell passed away in 1969, and through a complex set of purchases and land trades, the former Newhall estate has come into the hands of the U.S. Forest Service, which manages the property today as an historic site. A few interpretive signs have been placed near the home, outlining a bit of this scenic gem's history.

To find the trailhead for Skunk Harbor, drive north on Nevada State Highway 28, about 2.5-miles from its intersection with Highway 50 near Spooner Summit. Watch for a small parking area on the west side of the highway. Please note...if the parking area is full and you have to find an alternate spot, be sure to park in a safe, legal spot...fully off the road.

It's a 3-mile round-trip, 600' downhill hike to see Newhall's "picnic pavilion." The path is through a beautiful forest of pine, white fir, and incense cedar, some of which are 4' to 5' in diameter. The views of Lake Tahoe are, of course, stunning.

And how did Skunk Harbor get its name? Alternately, stories say a guest of Whittell had an encounter with several of the white striped creatures during a stay. Another story recounts how local law enforcement surprised guests at an illegal casino on the property, and how patrons scurried out of sight. As they later retold the story, they told how they had been "skunked" by the law.

The Newhalls maintained their "primary" Lake Tahoe residence, at Rubicon Pt. on the west shore.

Newhall's "picnic pavilion" at Skunk Harbor, makes a sizable estate in its own right.

Skunk Harbor as seen from the Lake. Notice in this photo from the 1920s, how the Tahoe hillsides are still pretty thin from the logging that occurred to support the Comstock mining of the 1860s-90s.

CHAPTER FOUR

LAKE TAHOE FREEWAY

(Or Bridge Over Emerald Bay)

Tales Along
LAKE TAHOE SHORES

If Lake Tahoe were thought to have a "crown jewel," there would be many who argue that it be Emerald Bay. The sublimity and pure beauty of this setting has warmed the hearts and souls of all (well…at least almost all) who have seen it since the dawn of humankind.

Emerald Bay can also be a formidable force of nature. In the winter of 1955, a large swath of dirt and rock above the Bay's south side gave way, plunging a large section of mountainside into the Lake. State Highway 89 was closed eleven months before repairs could be completed. The highway has always been a challenge to maintain. Snowslides and deep snows were common, often closing the winding mountain road for weeks at a time. After the 1955 slide, several Lake Tahoe area business leaders had had enough.

In the 1950s, many in the Tahoe business community saw great potential for dramatically increased growth supporting a booming, year-round, tourism-based economy. At the forefront of all this would be an improved system of highways including a "better route to get past Emerald Bay." Congress and President Eisenhower had started the massive Interstate Highway system, and building fast modern highways had come into vogue.

With the support of a few local lawmakers, the California State Division of Highways conducted studies, and had their engineers draw up plans for a modern four-lane thruway across Emerald Bay. The proposed route would come in low at current day Eagle Point Campground and cross the entrance to Emerald Bay on a low to the water, arched bridge. The route would then proceed north right through D.L. Bliss State Park. Highway Department officials even commissioned a watercolor artwork of Emerald Bay fronted by a bridge that appeared wistfully on the landscape. Opposition was immediate. Advocates for the bridge pointed out that San Francisco's Golden Gate Bridge was a beautiful piece of engineering, that actually drew people to visit it. One Tahoe summer resident wrote an editorial saying a bridge at Emerald Bay would provide drivers with stunning views and "could carry much more traffic with the result that the grandeur of Emerald Bay and the Rubicon area would become accessible to many, many more people than those who enjoy it now."

But most people were aghast at the proposal. State parks officials were adamantly opposed saying the bridge would not only mar the Emerald Bay landscape, but severely degrade D.L. Bliss State Park. Others said Emerald Bay was regal and worthy of no additional human intrusions.

The Emerald Bay Bridge was not the only major road project officials considered at the time. The state also proposed a wider and straighter mountain road above the Bay that would run through a long mountain tunnel. Some thought the tunnel proposal was a trick to draw attention away from the Emerald Bay Bridge project. A Sierra Club representative suggested state highway drawings made the scarring on the mountain route look worse, while making the bridge appear "toothpick size."

Low Level Emerald Bay Bridge Wins Support

SACRAMENTO. (Æ) — Construction of a low level highway and bridge across Emerald bay, Lake Tahoe, was endorsed by the senate finance committee Tuesday.

beauty comes above his love for his fellow senator, Swift Berry (R-Placerville).

Desmond spoke up against Berry's bill for a low level bridge across Lake Tahoe's Emerald bay, leading Berry to decide that

Despite intense opposition from some, the Emerald Bay Bridge also held support among many in the business community and several area politicians.

The idea of a new highway and Emerald Bay Bridge continued into the mid-1960's, but support of the project began to gradually lose steam. The League to Save Lake Tahoe, which was still in its infancy at the time, came out with both guns blazing in opposition. Their organized counterattack was very effective in educating the Tahoe loving public on the mega-highway proposal. The League's famous "Keep Tahoe Blue" rallying cry was coined at this time.

After Ronald Reagan was elected California Governor in 1966, he appointed William Penn Mott Jr. as his Director of State Parks. Mott was a trained landscape architect and career public land manager. He came out strongly against the Emerald Bay Bridge proposal, and he had Reagan's ear. Despite Reagan's earlier controversial public comment, "You know, a tree is a tree; how many more do you need to look at?" he realized the project's catastrophic ecological and political consequences, and officially ended the proposal. In his 1970 re-election campaign, Reagan would tout his "conservationism" in campaign ads, highlighting his opposition to the mega Tahoe Freeway. As a side note, William Mott went on to become President Reagan's Director of the National Park Service in 1985.

The League's effort brought additional attention to the rising effects of traffic and development on Lake Tahoe's greatest attribute, its water clarity. People who loved Lake Tahoe coalesced, and public attention became focused on Tahoe and the growing pressures it faced. In 1969, Emerald Bay was designated a National Natural Landmark for its illustrative character, rarity, diversity, and value to science and education.

Today, the narrow, winding highway above Emerald Bay remains much as it was in the winter of 1955-56. The state highway department (Caltrans) works hard to keep it open during even the biggest of Sierra storms. But

Mother Nature can still close it from time to time. And in summer, traffic can slow to a crawl as visitors wait for a parking spot in the small lot there. Fortunately, the Tahoe Basin never grew in the way some thought it would, and planners no longer focus on building bigger roads. Emphasis is now on finding ways to make it easier for more people in the coming years to park their cars, even outside the Basin, and take buses, hike, bike, and boat.

The fight over the Emerald Bay Bridge was a major landmark in Lake Tahoe's ecosystem. Though as a community, we can always do better in protecting Mother Nature's greatest temples, we can thank those that shouldered the good fight almost 70-years ago, for their efforts in protecting this sacred treasure we enjoy today.

The League to Save Lake Tahoe-Keep Tahoe Blue; https://www.keeptahoe-blue.org/

The proposed bridge (seen in this artist rendition) would have forever compromised one of the most celebrated views in the United States if not the world.

The huge rock slide that closed the highway around Emerald Bay in 1955 is visible center-left. This area is still prone to slides and avalanches today.

Fortunately, the view of Lake Tahoe and Emerald Bay is as sublime today as it has been for millennium.

CHAPTER FIVE

ON THIS LAND WE PUT OUR BRAND *"BONANZA"*

Odds are when one is asked what she/he associates with the Lake Tahoe area, clear water, deep forests, and soaring mountains are probable considerations. But in addition to these obvious associations, there is another term that comes to mind for many of us (or at least us oldsters) when we reflect upon what Lake Tahoe means to us...and that would be...*Bonanza*.

Debuting in 1959, Ben (Pa), Adam, Hoss, and Little Joe rode into the living rooms of American families with a breathtaking shot of Lake Tahoe revealed through a blazing map of their Ponderosa Ranch. The weekly series featured Lorne Greene as Ben Cartwright, the thrice widowed patriarch of a family of three boys: Pernell Roberts as Adam, Dan Blocker as Hoss, and Michael Landon as Little Joe.

The Cartwrights lived on their Ponderosa Ranch, located along Lake Tahoe's northeast shore. According to the TV map, their huge property extended to the outskirts of Minden on the southeast, Carson City to the east and the edge of Reno to the northeast. In season one-episode nine, Virginia City's Henry Comstock stated the Ponderosa was actually, "one thousand square miles," though a rough calculation of its size on the TV map indicates it would have been closer to two hundred square miles.

The series had a rough first season. Slotted against CBS' very popular *Perry Mason* on Saturday nights, *Bonanza* didn't even crack the top thirty watched shows that year. Several years later, actor Michael Landon confessed on the *Johnny Carson Show* that the entire film crew thought the original pilot was awful, and no one on the set gave it a chance. But things began to gel. The actors found their mark, the story lines developed, and NBC moved it to another time slot. It didn't hurt that color television manufacturer RCA owned NBC at the time, and was interested in selling more color TV sets (Bonanza was one of the first weekly series to be filmed in color).

A number of superlatives can be referenced in this legendary show. At 14 seasons and 432 episodes, it was the second-longest western in TV broadcast history (*Gunsmoke* is first). It had more viewers than any other show on television from 1964 to 1967 and remained in the top five for ten straight seasons. *TV Guide* ranks *Bonanza* as #43 on their Greatest TV Shows of All Time list.

Bonanza was considered an atypical western for its time, as the core of the storylines dealt less about the "range" but more with Ben and his three dissimilar sons, how they cared for one another, their neighbors, and doing right. *Bonanza* was the first series that was week-to-week about a family and the troubles it went through. *Bonanza* was a period drama that attempted to confront contemporary social issues. Episodes included subject matter on the environment, substance abuse, domestic violence, anti-war sentiment, and illegitimate births. And there were several episodes that sought to illustrate the cruelty and bigotry against Asians, Native Americans, Blacks, Jews, and the disabled. These themes were pretty groundbreaking at the time, when most networks and sponsors were worried about "stirring things up too much."

At first, all the outdoor scenes were filmed near Hollywood. The opening scene for the first season was filmed at Lake Hemet Reservoir, in the San Jacinto Mountains. It wasn't until later years the famous background of Lake Tahoe's Mt. Tallac and Bourne's Meadows/Nevada Beach was used. Most of the show's scenes were filmed in sound studios and back lots with only about twenty actual scenes ever filmed at the Lake over the series' fourteen seasons.

Starting in 1961, Crystal Bay contractor Bill Anderson was hired by the show's producers to cut roads and build fake outbuildings for a few exterior shots that were filmed around the Lake. In 1965, Anderson approached the show's producer David Dortort with the idea of building a replica of the Ponderosa Ranch house near Incline Village. With the financial backing and approval of Dortort as well as actors Greene, Landon, and Blocker, Anderson, turned his idea into a reality.

Lake Tahoe's "Ponderosa Ranch" opened to the public in 1968 with a replica of the Cartwright's home and barn. A likeness of Virginia City was later added. The *Bonanza* based theme park was wildly popular from the start. Anderson added numerous attractions including guests being "robbed by outlaws," horseback rides, wagon rides, a restaurant, souvenir shops, and tours of the ranch house. Visitors could even enjoy a "Hoss Burger" at the lunch counter. Anderson marketed the site for weddings and to small business groups. Even the James Beam Distilling Company held a sales and marketing convention there. As many as 250,000 people a summer would visit Lake Tahoe's Ponderosa Ranch.

Anderson's dream of having his Ponderosa used for filming of the TV show never materialized. The cost of shuttling actors and crew back and forth between Hollywood and Lake Tahoe would be cost prohibitive. NBC did however, shoot stock footage of the house and grounds, which were used intermittently in various episodes and the cast would make occasional promotional appearances.

In the early 2000s, visitation at the Ponderosa Ranch slowed, and in 2004, Anderson sold the property to a Silicon Valley businessman. Original plans called for the property to be developed into condominiums and homes, but as of 2023, the property remains mostly undeveloped.

The first Virginia City set used on the show from 1959–1970 was located on a back lot at Paramount Studios. It was also used in episodes of *Have Gun-Will Travel, Mannix,* and *The Brady Bunch.* In the 1970s *Bonanza* episode "The Night Virginia City Died," Deputy Clem Foster's pyromaniac fiancée leveled the town in a series of fires. This allowed for a switch to the "rebuilt Virginia City" less-expensive, Warner Brothers Studio's western set from September 1970 through the end of the show's run.

To fans' utter dismay, Pernell Roberts (Adam) left the show at the end of the 1964-65 season. Reportedly unhappy with the scripts and other issues with *Bonanza*, one of the things that annoyed Roberts the most was the relationship between Ben Cartwright and the three sons. Roberts talked about this with *The Washington Post* prior to leaving the show. "Isn't it just a bit silly for three adult males to get father's permission for everything they do? I have an important role. But everywhere I turn, there's the father image," he said.

Dan Blocker (Hoss) passed away unexpectedly following a routine gall bladder operation in 1972, which was ultimately one of the factors leading to the show's cancellation midway through season 14 in January 1973. Subsequently, the writers also had to make the tough decision to write Hoss off the show as they didn't wish to recast his character with anybody else. The show decided to give Hoss a heroic death with him drowning in an attempt to save a woman. His death didn't sit well with the mourning fans, as the show suffered from low viewership ratings thereafter. This nudged the writers to bring an end to the iconic show. The Hoss character's death also marked the first time in television history where a show dealt with an on-screen death.

Michael Landon (Little Joe) was only 22 when *Bonanza* first aired. He was very popular with the show's fans and worked his way in to write and even direct several *Bonanza* episodes. He of course went on to several years of success for his role as Charles Ingalls on the TV series *Little House on the Prairie* as well as Jonathon Smith in *Highway to Heaven*.

Lorne Greene, the Ben character, made his way west after a stint at sea. He was a formidable man, both in business (cattle, timber, mining) and politics. In one episode, he was asked to run for governor of Nevada. He was a loving but stern father, and his three boys meant more to him than anything else in life.

Many in Hollywood (actors and directors) at the time wanted to appear on the popular show with its pioneering social consciousness and storytelling. Famous Hollywood stars that made guest appearances included Ricardo Montalban, Caesar Romero, Adam West, Dennis Hopper, Sally Kellerman, Ron Howard, Leonard Nimoy, and dozens more.

Looking back at the stories that brought *Bonanza* to forefront of American culture in the 1960s and early '70s, many appear rather trite. The same plotlines that made *Bonanza* seem on the forefront of social justice in the early and mid-1960s, can seem uncomfortably patronizing today. But it is hard to argue with the decent and moral values the show continually brought into America's living rooms. And it is safe to say, *Bonanza* and the Cartwrights brought a much heightened consciousness (and appreciation) of beautiful Lake Tahoe to us all.

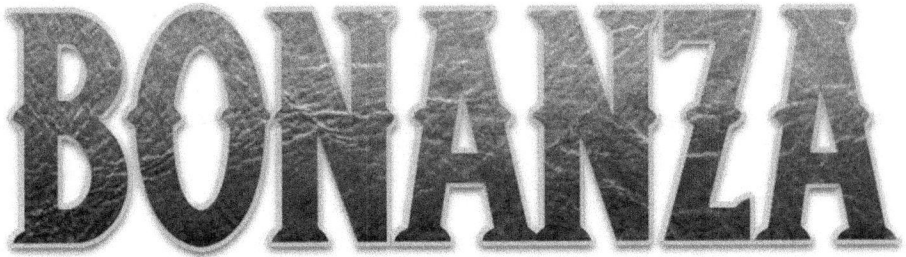

The image of the four Cartwrights galloping up the meadow, with beautiful Lake Tahoe in the background, is forever etched in our TV memories.

The Ponderosa Ranch was shown to be about the same size as Lake Tahoe on the show's classic map.

The original Bonanza cast L-R: Pernell Roberts (Adam), Dan Blocker (Hoss), Michael Landon (Little Joe), and Lorne Greene (Ben).

Due primarily to the high costs of transporting actors and crews...very few scenes from *Bonanza* were actually filmed on location at Lake Tahoe.

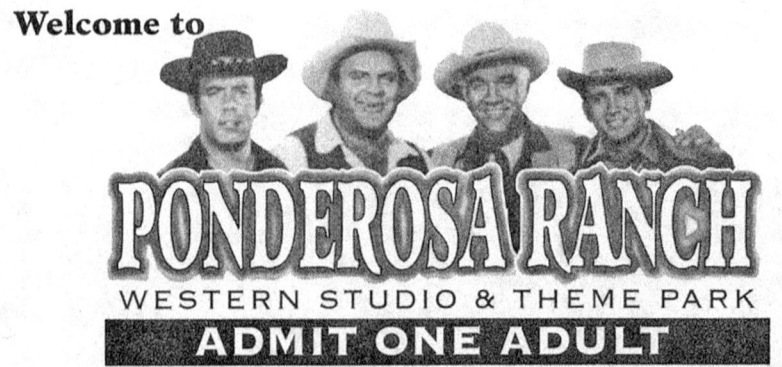

Welcome to

PONDEROSA RANCH
WESTERN STUDIO & THEME PARK
ADMIT ONE ADULT

Highway 28, North Shore Lake Tahoe
100 Ponderosa Ranch Rd.
Incline Village, NV 89451
(775) 831-0691

№ 756547

The Ponderosa Ranch "theme park" opened at Incline Village in 1968,
and continued for 30-years after *Bonanza* ended on television.
It attracted upwards of 250,000 people a year.

The "faux" Virginia City was one of the most popular attractions at the
Incline Village theme park.

Tales Along
LAKE TAHOE SHORES

CHAPTER SIX
FROZEN TOES AND TALL TALES
Captain Barter of Emerald Bay

"Captain" Richard Barter may have been the first "year-round" resident of Lake Tahoe. A retired British sea captain, Barter had roamed the western United States after retiring from the seven seas and settled upon the ocean like expanse of Lake Tahoe to call home. His place of residence was one of the most remote Tahoe area locales…Emerald Bay.

Ben Holladay had made a fortune in the transportation and express business. He was the founder and owner of the Overland Stage Company and became one of the wealthiest men in the United States by the 1860s. Holladay had made many trips past Lake Tahoe over the course of his work, and had always admired its beauty. While exploring the Lake in 1862, he came upon Emerald Bay and, soon after, filed claims on the land around the bay. He built one of the first private estates at Lake Tahoe and dubbed it "The Cottage." Captain Barter answered Holladay's ad for a year-round caretaker and spent the next 12 years living a reclusive life at this remote location.

Understandably, Barter would get lonely at his isolated abode. He would occasionally row his small skiff to Tahoe City and frequent the saloons in search of drink and companionship. He was often fairly inebriated on the return trip to Emerald Bay. In January of 1870, Barter was rowing back to his caretaker home when a gust of wind capsized his craft and tossed him into the frigid Lake Tahoe water.

Barter later recounted his ordeal to a newspaper reporter, "I knew it was useless to call for help…I also knew if I got in my boat and attempted to reach shore, I should certainly freeze to death." The good Captain claimed to have swam 10-miles to his cabin at Emerald Bay. According to Barter, when he climbed into his cabin, two of his toes were frozen stiff. To keep gangrene from setting in, he cut them off and placed the toes in a small jewelry box… which he always kept nearby. Barter loved to recount this story to anyone that would listen, and, if he was ever doubted, he would pull out his box and exclaim, "them's my toes!"

Apparently, the reality of his eventual mortality weighed heavily on Barter. Once sufficiently recovered, Barter carved out a small tomb with a coffin on Emerald Bay's Coquette (now Fannette) Island as his final resting place. There at his chosen spot near the island's summit rock, he also erected a small Gothic chapel with a sharply angled roof topped by a cross over the tomb. He told everyone this was where he wished to be buried.

While recovering from the self inflicted amputation of his toes, he constructed a seven foot scale model of a steam frigate, with every line, block and halyard in working order. Barter hand carved a crew of 225 figurines to populate his ship and even used a clock mechanism in the hold to turn the propeller. To move about while constructing the model, he tied cushions to his legs and "shoved around on his knees."

Captain Dick never tired of spinning tales (short and tall) about his life at Emerald Bay. A snow and rock avalanche crashed into the bay in 1868. The impact was so great, it drove two four-foot diameter sugar pines into the bottom of the bay like wharf pilings. He would always point these out as "what could have happened to him."

The good Captain had a reputation for enjoying intoxicating beverages. When questioned by a reporter for the *Cincinnati Commercial* about his frequent imbibing, Barter was quoted, "Do you think comrade, that a man can spend his life upon this pond {Tahoe}, among these snow steeples, and not have a spree now and then? There's too much ice water in the Sierrys for a man to be a temperance chap. Why...Tahoe means 'lager beer.' Ho for Emerald Bay! Damn my eyes! Let's all drink...hurray!"

Despite his careful preparations building his final resting place, Barter never made it to the tomb. While rowing home one night after another Tahoe City "evening" in 1873, his dinghy was again caught in a wild Lake Tahoe gale. His small craft was tossed about in the Lake's icy waters, flipping over and flinging Barter once again into the frigid inland sea. This time, he never made it back into his boat. His body was never found.

The little chapel and tomb were removed by later owners. Legendary Emerald Bay resident and the force behind the famous Vikingsholm, Lora Josephine Knight, had her Tea House constructed on Fannette Island. The stone structure has been part of the Emerald Bay landscape now for almost 100 years.

In the year following Barter's demise, Captain "Jack Tar" Sweetser took over the position as caretaker at Holladay's Emerald Bay property. In 1877, Captain Jack became a legendary character of Emerald Bay in his own right, thanks in part to the famous Jehu (stagecoach driver) of the Sierra, Hank Monk (see chapter twenty-five). When Emerald Bay froze over in the winter of 1877-78, Monk saw an opportunity to add new incredulous laurels to his already colorful reputation.

After the Bay had froze, Monk quietly spread the story around Carson City that fishing had become a major winter industry at Lake Tahoe. Hank told of how miners, under the direction of Captain "Jack Tar," were driving shafts and tunnels through the frozen bay, and harvesting native cutthroat and silver trout with great success. Monk said he had purchased stock in the "fish claim" and was expecting substantial dividends. He estimated there was 100 tons of trout imprisoned in the ice of Emerald Bay and that "Old Jack" and his associates would be working nonstop to harvest the catch before things thawed out. The *Nevada Appeal* bannered the story under the heading "Trout Mining at Lake Bigler" (Tahoe's original name).

Emerald Bay has certainly inspired a good deal of artists, poets, and photographers over the years. It appears this beautiful gem of Mother Nature has also inspired a fair share of tellers of tall tales as well. Maybe it's something in the water...

Captain Barter, shown with his dog, also loved to build model sailing ships.

Captain Barter built his own tomb topped by a small chapel on the top of Emerald Bay's Fannette Island after his brush with death on Lake Tahoe's frigid waters.

IMPRESS YOUR FRIENDS
WITH WHAT YOU KNOW!

Lake Tahoe is the sixth largest U.S. lake by volume (behind the five Great Lakes). It is 12-miles wide, 22-miles long, and 1,645 feet at its deepest. According to the Desert Research Institute of Nevada, measurements of evaporation rates at the Lake indicate that 36 inches of water evaporate from the Lake annually, or 0.1 inch per day. This equals about 330-million gallons a day, which is greater than the water that flows out of Lake Tahoe via the Truckee River in the same time period.

Lake Tahoe is old...over 2-million years old, making it one of the oldest lakes in the world.

The water of Lake Tahoe has been tested as 99.994% pure, which is cleaner than most commercially distilled water. In fact, water suppliers who draw from deep within the lake aren't even required to filter it before delivering the water to local customers.

The Lake is renown for its beautiful blue color. The previous fact about Lake Tahoe is actually what contributes to it's lovely blue color. Water as pure as Tahoe will absorb red light on the color spectrum. When clear skies shine on the lake, the red is absorbed, leaving a clear blue color.

Sixty-three tributaries flow into Lake Tahoe. Despite this abundance of "inflow"...about half the water that enters Lake Tahoe every year, does so by rain and snow falling directly into the Lake.

Because of Lake Tahoe's large surface area and immense depth, it contains a staggering volume of water. Theoretically, Lake Tahoe contains enough water to supply every person in the United States with 50-gallons of water every day for five years.

Fleur de Lac, an estate near Homewood, was featured in the 1974 epic film–The Godfather Part II. Many iconic scenes were filmed at the estate, including the assassination attempt on Michael, Carmela Corleone's funeral, Fredo's execution when he's fishing, and the legendary closing scene of Michael sitting outside all by himself. The estate was originally built by wealthy industrialist Henry Kaiser of Kaiser Steel.

Lake Tahoe has three different earthquake fault lines. The West Shore fault, the Stateline fault and the Incline Village fault.

CHAPTER SEVEN

HIGH STAKES IN THE HIGH SIERRA

The Kidnapping of Frank Sinatra Jr.

Tales Along
LAKE TAHOE SHORES

There have been many bizarre stories of true crime in the annals of human transgressions. In 1963, one of the more unusual acts of criminality originated near the shores of enchanted Lake Tahoe.

During November of 1963, two 23-year-old former high school class-mates, Barry Keenan and Joe Amsler (soon joined by a third conspirator-John Irwin), followed 19-year old Frank Sinatra Jr. as he made his way from city to city on a concert tour. Sinatra Jr. was being promoted by his legend-ary father as the next singing sensation. Keenan and Amsler had hatched a plan to kidnap "Old Blue Eyes'" son, and hold him for a sizable ransom from his wealthy father.

On December 8, 1963, Sinatra Jr. was at Stateline's Harrah's Club, having been booked to perform in their showroom with the Tommy Dorsey Band. Around 9 PM, Keenan and Amsler knocked on Junior's door at his motel room pretending to be delivering a package. They bound and blindfolded his friend John Foss (who was also in the room) and hustled Junior out to the trunk of their car.

Frank Sinatra Jr. was kidnapped from his South Lake Tahoe motel room on the evening of December 8, 1963.

25

Within minutes, Foss was able to free himself and notify casino security. Law enforcement officers quickly set up roadblocks in an attempt to intercept the perpetrators. The kidnappers were even stopped in one, but deluded the officers with a concocted story as they headed to their Southern California hideout.

By 9:40 PM, the FBI had joined the search and soon met with Sinatra Sr. who had flown to Reno after learning of the kidnapping. The G-Men thought the kidnappers would demand a ransom from Sinatra Sr. Plans were laid out for the money to be paid, and the FBI would track the money and find the kidnappers. On the morning of December 9, the kidnappers reached Sinatra Sr. by phone and instructed him to go to Ron's Filling Station in Carson City for further instructions. The kidnappers demanded that all further communication be conducted by payphone. During these conversations, Frank Sr. became concerned that he would not have enough coins for the calls, which prompted him to carry 10 dimes with him at all times for the rest of his life. It is said he was even buried with 10 dimes in his pocket! The kidnappers told Sr. to get to Southern California and await further instructions.

On December 10, with Sinatra Jr. being held in Canoga Park, kidnapper Irwin called Sinatra Sr. again, demanding $240,000 in ransom, with instructions to drop it off at a Wilshire Blvd. filling station between two parked school buses.

Roadblocks were quickly set up during a Lake Tahoe winter storm. The kidnappers were even stopped, but deluded the officers with a concocted story.

The drop was made during the early morning hours of December 11. Irwin stood guard over Junior while Keenan and Amsler picked up the money. But Irwin had gotten nervous and set Sinatra Jr. free. An unharmed Junior was walking through an exclusive Bel-Air neighborhood when found at about 3:00 AM by a private security guard.

The pressure was too much, and Irwin broke down. He spilled the beans to his brother, who immediately called police. The three kidnappers were soon arrested, and all the money recovered just a few hours after Junior was released.

The kidnappers' defense attorney concocted a story that Sinatra Jr. had arranged the kidnapping himself as a publicity stunt to help boost his career. A jury wasn't buying it, and the trio were convicted and sentenced to life in prison, though all three ended up serving less than five years.

Convicted kidnappers L-R: Barry Keenan, Joe Amsler, and John Irwin.

A few peculiar side notes to the kidnapping:

Kidnapper Barry Keenan had been a grade school classmate of Nancy Sinatra, Frank Jr.'s sister, when he was younger. In an interview with the New York Times conducted years after he had been released from prison(1998), Keenan explained that after a car accident had caused a back injury and left him in chronic pain, he became addicted to Percodan, muscle relaxers, and tranquilizers. His addiction bankrupted him, and so he devised a plan to kidnap Frank Jr. for ransom—which he claimed he would have invested, and later return the ransom money when he was back on his feet.

Keenan went on to say he had considered kidnapping the son of Bob Hope, but thought that would be "un-American." He also thought the son of tough guy Sinatra Sr. would "handle" the stressful situation better.

And shortly after Sinatra Jr.'s kidnapping became public, reputed Chicago Mob Boss and acquaintance of Sinatra Sr., Sam Giancana, offered his "personal assistance" in resolving the kidnapping. Sinatra declined Giancana's offer and went with the FBI.

Frank Sinatra Junior's career never did make it to the level of his acclaimed father. Over his life's work, he sang, acted a little, and even worked as his father's musical director towards the end of Senior's career. Frank Sinatra Jr. passed away in March of 2016.

Alleged Chicago Mob Boss Sam Giancana (L) offered his "personal assistance" to Frank Sinatra to help resolve his son's kidnapping. Frank Sr. declined.

Harrahs Club Lake Tahoe in the late 1950s.

CHAPTER EIGHT

OLYMPIC TRAINING AT LAKE TAHOE
Track and Field at Echo Summit

Many people are aware of Lake Tahoe's association with the 1960 Winter Olympics that were held at Squaw Valley, California. The event brought huge amounts of exposure of Lake Tahoe to a worldwide audience. The 1960 Winter Olympics literally put the Lake Tahoe area on the map…especially when it came to winter sports.

But, the Lake Tahoe area enjoyed a partnership with another Olympic event, though not as well-known as the '60 Winter Olympics. Big Blue's contribution to the success of the U.S. team in that year's summer Olympic event is interesting, significant, and historic.

In 1963, the International Olympic Committee announced that Mexico City was chosen as the site of the 1968 Summer Olympics. These would be the first Olympic Games to be held in Latin America and the first to be staged in a Spanish-speaking country. They were also the first Games to exclusively use electronic timekeeping equipment for all events.

The '68 Olympics would be the "highest" Summer Olympics ever held. Mexico City sits at 7,349-feet above sea level, which provides about 23% less oxygen than at sea level. There was a good deal of concern what affects the oxygen deprived air would have on the athletes and their performances. The U.S. Olympic High Altitude Training Committee was established to formulate a plan and secure a location for a high-elevation training camp for the U.S. athletes.

Walt Little was the Recreation Director for the City of South Lake Tahoe at the time. He had also been the sports editor of the *Bakersfield Californian* and editor of the *Lake Tahoe News*. Little had made a lot of connections over the years and happened to know well, Payton Jordan, the longtime track coach at Stanford who would lead the 1968 U.S. Olympic men's team.

Little's son had worked at the Echo Summit ski resort (now known as Adventure Mountain Lake Tahoe) that winter. Over dinner conversation one night, Little Jr. reminded his father that Echo Summit was almost the exact same elevation as Mexico City, and that it might serve as a perfect spot for the U.S. athletes to train. Little called his friend Jordan with this idea, and Jordan replied, "You are insane, Little. When do we start?" The two began making phone calls.

Little asked St. Cloud State coach Bob Tracy, who had supervised an altitude training study for the USOC in 1967, to accompany him on a jeep ride through the mountains surrounding Lake Tahoe. St. Cloud was impressed and lent his support to a Lake Tahoe Olympic training site. What started as dinner conversation, snowballed into an avalanche of support…and the USOC chose Lake Tahoe as its 1968 Summer Olympics training site.

Tahoe Sought as Site For Olympic Training

Gazette-Journal
Carson City Bureau

Representatives from Nevada and California meet tonight at South Lake Tahoe in hopes of having the area designated as the U.S. Olympic training site.

"There is a definite need to train in altitude comparable to where the team will be competing," University of Nevada track coach Dick Dankworth said today.

He said the 7,000-plus Lake Tahoe altitude is roughly the same as in Mexico City, where hundreds of U.S. athletes are expected to compete in the 1968 Olympics.

"Medical and physiological research has proven there are effects that take place within the human body which require individuals to acclimate," Dankworth said.

The meeting will be held at the Tahoe Sands Motel at Stateline, Nev. beginning at 6 p.m. The move was prompted, in part, by South Lake Tahoe Mayor Norman Woods.

Nevada is one of four sites under consideration as a training area. Others are in Wyoming, Colorado and New Mexico.

Dankworth said it will be up to the U.S. Olympic Committee to make the final site selection.

Dankworth, who was asked to attend the meeting by Gov. Paul Laxalt, said about four weeks is needed to acclimate the athletes.

"That's about the minimum time," he said. "Many groups recommend the athletes stay in high altitude until the last possible time."

The reason, Dankworth said, is that athletes will be faced with intestinal disorders as soon as they arrive in Mexico City.

"This will kill a guy who is running," Dankworth said of expected food and water problems. He said this was particularly true of distance runners.

In 1967, South Tahoe was chosen as the training site for the 1968 U.S. Olympic Team.

The citizens and business leaders of South Lake Tahoe understood what hosting the Olympic athletes would mean. South Tahoe would be the center of the track and field universe for ten weeks. The entire South Tahoe community came together to make the dream a reality. In addition to the financial contribution made by the city itself, citizen groups and committees raised money through different fund-raising activities. A "U.S. Olympic Benefit Basketball Tournament" was held at South Tahoe High School. The South Lake Tahoe Soroptimist Club donated money toward underwriting the purchase of hurdles, and a benefit banquet was held in the High Sierra Room of Sahara Tahoe (now Hard Rock Casino).

Four hundred-twenty people attended the $10 per person fundraising banquet. Actor Van Heflin attended the event and proclaimed, "I'm sure you're all proud of the aggressive leadership that made this possible. It just didn't happen accidentally."

A permit would be required to construct a track and field training site at the Echo Summit Ski Area. The U.S. Forest Service approved the permit for the temporary construction of a 400-meter oval track and ancillary facilities in the middle of the forest, on top of Echo Summit. The main concern of the Forest Service was that the site should be disturbed as little as possible. Only trees that "had" to be cut down were permitted to be removed…which led for some rather "unusual" conditions.

A row of bleachers that could seat 350 people lined the finish line straight away. Some spectators climbed on nearby rocks or hillsides to watch the events. The start of the 200-meter dash was completely obstructed by trees.

The javelin and hammer throw circles were also shrouded in trees within the track. "You damn near had to aim to miss the trees," said U.S. hammer throw athlete Ed Burke. "The long jump runway came right out of the woods. The long jump pit itself was near the finish line, but jumpers began their approach obscured from view by a forest of pines. The high jump pit was surrounded by huge granite boulders."

The track at the Echo Summit training facility was partially hidden in the pine trees.

With Harrah's Tahoe casino offering support, and with revenue raised from a five-cent motel tax, South Lake Tahoe officials were able to buy and install a synthetic "Tartan" track modeled along the specific lines of the track that would be used at Mexico City. At that time, most outdoor tracks were made of an earth or cinder surface. Rain and use would cause a track to break down and become "slow," and runner's times often showed it. The 3-M Company developed the Tartan track. It was unaffected by weather or athletes' spikes, and for the first time, runners were able to count on a track as fast on the last day of competition as on the first.

The state-of-the-art track had a distinctive pink color. The Forest Service required the track be removed once the trials and training were completed. It was relocated to South Lake Tahoe Middle School, where it proudly served its student athletes for many years.

1968 was a time of great social turmoil in the United States. In addition to the divisiveness among Americans from the Vietnam War, there was a great deal of civil unrest in the country as well. The Reverend Dr. Martin Luther King was assassinated in April of that year, followed two months later by the murder of Robert Kennedy.

Sprinters Tommie Smith, Lee Evans, and John Carlos were leaders of the "Olympic Project for Human Rights," a movement initiated by Harry Edwards, a sociology professor at San Jose State, where Smith and Evans were students. Plans for an Olympic boycott by black athletes had been in the works since 1967, but had begun to wane by the time training started at Echo Summit. Nonetheless, the issues of the day weighed heavily over America's psyche.

During that summer of Tahoe training, tensions seemed to relax, and camaraderie among the athletes grew. Carlos, who was born and raised in Harlem, said he adapted quickly to the mountain setting, which he remembered fondly.

"The first thing I remember about Tahoe is how unique that facility was," he said. "It was very scenic and relaxing. And then I remember certain times it would snow. I remember the treacherous rides up and down that hill, with all the turns and so forth. And then I remember that it made the team a lot closer. I think the team bonded. It was such a serene atmosphere. I think everyone just fell in love with the place and the situation."

1968 Olympic Decathlon gold medalist Bill Toomey also enjoyed the Tahoe training facility. When it was time to leave South Tahoe and head to Mexico City, Toomey and many other athletes were greatly saddened. "The town went out of its way to take care of us. Nobody wanted to leave," Toomey said. "It was a very strange feeling being downbeat going to the Olympics, which should have been our highest point emotionally."

There must have been something special in the air that summer at Echo Summit. Three world records were set, and the men's team went on to set six more records in Mexico City. Many say the 1968 U.S. Men's Olympic Team was the best ever assembled. The U.S. won 45 gold medals at Mexico City.

In June of 2017, 11 members of that team returned to the Echo Summit training area to commemorate the site which had been declared a California Historic Landmark.

Today at Echo Summit, the paved outline of a track can still be seen in the parking lot serving Adventure Mountain Lake Tahoe. Echo Summit is also a trailhead for the Pacific Coast National Scenic Trail, where hikers and backpackers blissfully enter the Lake Tahoe backcountry. The magic and inspiration of beautiful Echo Summit...lives on.

A few of the 1968 Olympic athletes who trained at Echo Summit- South Lake Tahoe.

CHAPTER NINE

LAKE OF
MANY USES
A History of Echo Lakes

When gold was first discovered in the California foothills in 1848, prospectors retrieved the precious metal from streams and riverbeds using simple techniques, such as panning. As the surface gold was played out, prospectors figured out that the banks and hillsides of the creeks and rivers most likely were laden with the precious yellow mineral as well. They were right.

The quickest and easiest method to extract the gold held in the dirt and gravels was to wash away the earth with water under high pressure and direct it down into sluices for panning. Hydraulic mining was first used in 1853, and its use grew as the "easy found" gold on the surface dwindled.

In 1873, John Kirk and F.A. Bishop dammed and rose the depth of Echo Lake, near current day Echo Pass off Highway 50. The outflow from the Echo Lakes (there is an upper and a lower) naturally flowed east into Lake Tahoe, but Kirk and Bishop built a diversion canal, bringing the water west down the South Fork of the American River's drainage. The water from the Echo Lakes was used to support the hydraulic mining for gold near Placerville.

The original diversion canal fought an "uphill battle" getting water from Echo Lakes over to the American River. In 1876, Chinese laborers were used to drill a 1,058' tunnel from the lakes, under and through the granite of Echo Summit to the American River drainage.

Seeing the devastating affect hydraulic mining was having on the land, California's first environmental law was passed in 1884, outlawing hydraulic mining throughout the state.

The Echo Lake diversion system no longer had work to perform. But with the infrastructure already in place, other business possibilities were quickly recognized. Over the next few decades, Echo Lakes' water was used to augment domestic water supplies, generate electricity, and eventually irrigate farmlands west of Placerville, which it still does today.

There are additional features that are part of the Echo Lakes water diversion system. Aloha, Ralston, Lake of the Woods, Ropi, and a few other lakes in Desolation Wilderness are all dammed with their outflows regulated. These controlled flows help maintain the available water for the Placerville area through the summer and fall. The level of the Echo Lakes is mandated to remain at a certain elevation through Labor Day by the U.S. Forest Service so that the water taxi can continue to operate during the hiking season.

Upper and Lower Echo Lakes remain a very popular location in the Lake Tahoe area. It is a primary trailhead for hikers and backpackers entering Desolation Wilderness. There is a small resort at Lower Echo Lake that operates a water taxi service, allowing hikers to cut 2 miles (one way) off their hike into

Desolation's beautiful backcountry.

The Echo Lakes are located about 2.25-miles northwest of Echo Summit off U.S. Hwy. 50. GPS coordinates: 38.83495, -120.044585.

Upper and Lower Echo Lakes have been providing water to the Placerville area for over 150 years.

As early as 1873, water was brought all the way from Echo Lake (near Lake Tahoe) to provide water for hydraulic mining near Placerville.

Tales Along
LAKE TAHOE SHORES

CHAPTER TEN
SAVE THE OLD GROWTH FOREST
Lucky Baldwin at Lake Tahoe

The list of colorful characters who have helped shape the human history of Lake Tahoe is long and engaging. Entrepreneurs, politicians, conservationists, and boosters of all types of men and women have engaged in the business that is Lake Tahoe over the years. Elias (Lucky) J. Baldwin is one of those that has worn many different hats over his time at the Lake.

Baldwin was born in Ohio. In his youth, he was known to be strong willed, a wanderer, and adventurer. Tempted by the many stories of easy riches, he came west in 1853 when he was only 25 years of age. Settling in San Francisco, he opened a hotel that did quite well. He took those profits and invested wisely in mining stocks. In one business transaction, he received 2,000 shares in Virginia City's Ophir Mine, which at the time had a very low valuation. But soon enough, the Ophir's deposit of silver proved to be one of the richest of the Comstock, and Baldwin's wealth increased multifold.

According to one account, he may have earned the nickname Lucky while on an overseas trip. The story goes, that before he left for his trip, Baldwin instructed his stockbroker to sell the shares of a certain stock when it reached $800. When the stock hit Baldwin's price, the broker was unable to sell it because the stock certificates were locked in a safe, and Baldwin had taken the key to Europe. The price of the stock continued to climb, and, by the time Lucky Baldwin returned to the U.S., the stock had gone up from $800 to about $10,000 a share. "Lucky" indeed!

Baldwin first saw Lake Tahoe while on a pack trip shortly after his arrival in the Golden State. Over the next few years, he visited the Lake often, as he traveled to and from Virginia City to check on his mining interest. He was impressed by Tahoe's scenic value and thought there were commercial opportunities as well.

One of his favorite stopping points was Yank's Resort near present day Meyers. Yank's owner Ephraim "Yank" Clement owned over 1,000 acres of mostly forested land. He had resisted the attempts of lumbermen to harvest his trees as they were fast removing virtually all the other timber of the Tahoe Basin. The Comstock Lode had a voracious appetite for lumber and fuel wood, and Clement's old trees were some of the few that had not fallen victim to the ax.

Even the profit driven Baldwin was astonished by the de-forestation taking place in the Tahoe area. He reportedly exclaimed to Clement, "By Gad! It's a shame and a crime! Someone will be cutting this timber next," waving his hand at Yank's magnificent forest.

In 1881, Baldwin purchased Clement's property, and acquired an additional 7,000 acres of adjacent lands. He often bragged that the lumberman's ax would never be seen on his lands and that he had "saved" Lake Tahoe's last vestige of virgin forest.

As altruistic as his motives may have appeared, it was not as if there wasn't any commercial bent to Baldwin's Tahoe acquisitions. His land purchases included a waystation/hotel, which he christened the Tallac Point House. With significant improvements to the modest property, Baldwin changed the clientele from every day working men and women to the well to do of San Francisco and Virginia City.

With the tourism business increasing at his small hotel, Baldwin began construction in 1899 on a larger, more luxurious resort, the grand Tallac Hotel. It was three-and-a half stories high, with a tower, a covered porch and boasted indoor plumbing and heating. Patrons enjoyed an eight-course dinner while an orchestra played in the background. A week's stay at the Tallac cost $32.50, at a time when most people earned around $80 a month. Women of the upper class would stroll along a lighted walkway dubbed the Promenade as it wound through the magnificent grounds.

Despite its opulence, getting to Baldwin's Tallac Hotel was not an easy affair. Guests would take the train to Truckee, then a stage to Tahoe City. From there, Baldwin's steamer *The Tallac* would transport the excited passengers across Lake Tahoe to his south shore property. Baldwin built his own home around two old-growth Jeffrey Pines, symbolizing his respect for the old trees.

The resort was a success, and Baldwin added a waterfront casino to the property in 1902. Gaming was illegal in California, but Baldwin relied on friends and acquaintances in Placerville to let him know when the sheriff was coming up to the Lake for a visit. By the time the sheriff would arrive, staff had hidden the slots and roulette wheels out of sight.

Baldwin's Tallac Hotel drew a full house nearly every night during the summer. It remained his pride and joy, even as he spent more and more time developing his real estate interests in the Los Angeles metropolitan area.

Lucky Baldwin was a major player in the development of Southern California. He had purchased over 63,000 acres of the San Gabriel Valley in 1875, and, as the Southland grew, Baldwin subdivided much of the property into lots for sale. The towns of Arcadia, Monrovia, and Sierra Madre are all made up of land originally owned by Baldwin. A portion of his property became Baldwin Hills.

Baldwin also had a keen interest in thoroughbred race horses and built the original Santa Anita Racetrack in 1905. The grandstand burned down, but his daughter Anita built the current track on property just to the west. Prestigious Santa Anita Racetrack is still providing a world class horse racing experience.

Baldwin was married four times, with the first three marriages ending in divorce. His third and fourth wives were both only 16 when they wedded Baldwin. He and his fourth wife separated after less than two years but never divorced. Over his lifetime, he was sued by four women for breach of promise of marriage. One of the jilted suitors shot and wounded him in 1883. He also narrowly escaped death in a San Francisco courtroom on July 2, 1896. He was being sued by Lillian Ashley for seduction, and, while she was on the witness stand, her sister Emma Ashley walked up behind Baldwin and fired a pistol at him grazing his skull.

His stature as a celebrity was such that at age 56, when he wedded his fourth wife in San Francisco, the wedding drew coast-to-coast press coverage. In the same year, he was sued by a jilted 16-year-old girl who the courts eventually awarded $75,000 in damages.

Lucky Baldwin passed away in 1907. After his death, his estate was managed by his longtime friend and advisor Hiram A. Unruh. Land owned by the estate was not worth much upon his death, but ten years later, oil was discovered on the property. This became the Montebello Oil Fields, which would produce one-eighth of the crude-oil in California, one of the biggest oil fields in the west.

Lucky Baldwin was many things over his lifetime. Some say scoundrel, some say a cheat, or maybe an egocentric tightwad. We will leave that for others to debate. But one thing is certain, Lucky Baldwin helped bring the beauty of Lake Tahoe into the age of tourism…and his love of giant old growth trees has left us a legacy of one of the most beautiful forests in the Lake Tahoe Basin.

Much of Baldwin's old growth Tahoe forest can be seen at the Tallac Historic Site on Hwy. 89, just a few miles west of the Y at South Lake Tahoe. GPS coordinates: 38.93941, -120.04675.

Lucky Baldwin was one of the earliest promoters of tourism at Lake Tahoe.

Lucky Baldwin's Tallac House, on Lake Tahoe's south shore, attracted visitors from throughout the world. Baldwin operated a casino here which escaped the knowledge of the local sheriff for many years.

Lucky Baldwin's Lake Tahoe legacy lives on today in the beautiful old growth forest at Lake Tahoe's Tallac Historic Site.

CHAPTER ELEVEN

THE PONY EXPRESS AT LAKE TAHOE

Tales Along
LAKE TAHOE SHORES

The Pony Express made an indelible mark upon the mysticism of the American West. Though short lived, its place in western myth and lore is forever set for the annals of time.

The idea of having a fast mail route to the Pacific Coast was prompted largely by California becoming an integral part of the Union after the discovery of gold in 1848. By 1860, there were 380,000 people living in California. The demand for a faster way to get the mail and other communications to and from this important, westernmost state became even greater as the American Civil War approached.

William Russell, Alexander Majors, and William B. Waddell were the three founders of the Pony Express. They were already in the freighting business and had over 6,000 employees, owned 75,000 oxen, horses, and mules, thousands of wagons, warehouses, plus a sawmill, a meatpacking plant, a bank, and an insurance company.

By using the shortest route and mounted riders rather than traditional stagecoaches, they proposed to establish a fast mail service between St. Joseph, Missouri, and Sacramento, California, with letters delivered in 10 days, which many said was impossible. The initial price was set at $5 per 1/2 ounce but eventually dropped to $1. The Pony Express was not part of the U.S. Mail, rather a private carrier much like UPS or FedEx. The founders of the Pony Express hoped to win an exclusive government mail contract, but that never came about.

Russell, Majors, and Waddell organized and put together the Pony Express in just two months during the winter of 1860. The undertaking assembled 80 riders, 184 stations, 400 horses, and several hundred personnel in just the first two months of 1861. In order to keep the horse's load as light as possible, only men of slender stature were hired.

One of the most important of the 184 stations was at Lake Tahoe. Within site of the hustle and bustle of the gaming action at Stateline, Nevada, stands a little known but extraordinary piece of Lake Tahoe area history. The two-and-one-half story, white, wood frame building is known as Friday's Station. It has sat on the high ground just a bit northeast of the current Stateline casino area for over 160 years. The stately building features eight white columns supporting a two-tiered veranda. Architects consider it a western adaptation of Greek Revival design. The beautiful structure is in very good condition and has been excellently maintained over the years.

Friday's Station near Stateline, is the only original and fully intact Pony Express station still standing in Nevada.

Originally built about 1858 by Friday Burke and James Small as a stage-station on the Placerville-Carson City Road, Friday's became an important home station for the Pony Express when the fabled outfit began carrying the mail in April of 1860. This was the first home station on the Pony Express route for riders coming from Sacramento heading east. One of the Pony Express' most famous riders was the relay rider based at Friday's, Robert (Pony Bob) Halsam. He is credited with having made the longest uninterrupted ride during the brief duration of the Pony Express.

Pony Bob's route would take him east 75 miles to Buckland Station on the Carson River (near current day Silver Springs, NV). Hostilities between local Paiute and Washo Native Americans, and Euro-settlers had broken out in the region. Signal fires were blazing when Pony Bob rode in to a relay station 60-miles from Lake Tahoe. Settlers had taken all of the horses at the station for use in the campaign against the Native Americans, leaving Bob with no fresh mount. And when he arrived at Buckland's 15 miles further, the relief rider was so frightened, he refused to take the mail from Bob.

Pony Bob changed mounts at Buckland's, and, within ten minutes, rode on over a long dry stretch of trail. Finally, after 190 miles in the saddle, Bob turned the mail pouches over to J.G. Kelly at Smith Creek. In less than nine hours, Bob was headed back west. He made his way back to Friday's without a mishap after a hard 380-mile round trip ride. He was only four hours off the Pony Express' set schedule when he arrived back at Friday's.

The transcontinental telegraph line put an end to the Pony Express by October of 1861. During the 1870s through the 1880s, Friday's operated as a resort under the name Buttermilk Bonanza Ranch, offering "the finest hunting, fishing, and general well-being to be found in the Tahoe Region."

Bob relocated to Idaho and continued as an express rider and later, a stage driver. He worked for a time as an Army scout and a U.S. Marshall. Bob became friends with Buffalo Bill Cody, and is said to have helped arrange the surrender of Sitting Bull.

In the 1890s, David Brooks Park acquired Friday's Station, as well as several hundred acres of prime land at Nevada Stateline. Friday's was used as the summer headquarters for the family's cattle business, grazing up to 200 head on the beautiful Sierra pastureland up until the 1960s. Park also built an ice

PONY EXPRESS
St. JOSEPH, MISSOURI to CALIFORNIA
in 10 days or less.

YOUNG, SKINNY, WIRY FELLOWS

not over eighteen. Must be expert riders, willing to risk death daily.

Orphans preferred.
Wages $25 per week.

APPLY, PONY EXPRESS STABLES
St. JOSEPH, MISSOURI

A help wanted ad for hiring Pony Express riders.

house and butcher shop where the Harvey's Casino parking structure sits today.

The Park family still owns a substantial amount of property in the Stateline area, including the magnificent five-star Edgewood Tahoe Resort and Golf Course.

Today, Friday's Station is the only fully intact, original Pony Express Station in Nevada still standing and is listed on the National Register of Historic Places.

Please note...Friday's Station is on private property and is not open to the public. Please be respectful and do not trespass.

Friday's Station near Stateline in the late 1800s.

Tales Along
LAKE TAHOE SHORES

CHAPTER TWELVE
LARGER THAN LIFE
Unconventional George Whittell

"Sometimes the best things in life are accidents that go right."
Elizabeth Lowel

Lake Tahoe is among the brightest jewels in the crown of Mother Nature, while at the same time one of the most heavily visited destinations in California. Development at certain parts of the Lake resembles a bustling metropolis more than a mountain village.

Thankfully though, large portions of Lake Tahoe do remain undeveloped. Primarily on the northeast and southwest shores, the U.S. Forest Service, and the Nevada and California State Park systems manage thousands of acres of near pristine Lake Tahoe beauty.

The eight miles of Lake Tahoe shoreline between Sand Harbor and Glenbrook remain "almost" completely without development. It is the largest stretch of unspoiled lakefront at "Big Blue." How did such a large tract of some of the most valuable real estate imaginable remain unspoiled? Can we thank Pa Cartwright and the boys for keeping this region, once known (at least in TV land) as the Ponderosa, unsullied? Not quite. Though the fictitious property did indeed appear on studio maps in this exact location on Tahoe's NE shore, the story of the untrammeled lands of Lake Tahoe is so peculiar, even the best TV script writers couldn't top this one.

George Whittell Jr. was born in San Francisco in 1881, the only son in one of San Francisco's wealthiest families. His maternal grandfather was one of the founders of PG&E, the Northern California utility corporation, and owned many other businesses as well. George was the sole heir to his family's inheritance when they had passed away. The estate was worth hundreds of millions of dollars at today's exchange. George was smart and shrewd. He sold off the family's stock holdings and converted it to cash just a few months before the 1929 Wall Street Crash. When others were financially destitute, George Whittell Jr. had his family's assets safely converted to cash.

"Captain" Whittell, as he liked to be called, is quoted as saying, "When men stop boozing, womanizing, and gambling, the bloom is off the rose." Whittell began his oppositional antics at quite an early age, running away with the Barnum & Bailey Circus after high school rather than attending college, eloping with a chorus girl rather than settling down with a society bride his parents had planned for him, and volunteering with the Italian and French armies years before the U.S. entered World War I.

The Whittell estate was located on the hills near Palo Alto in an area now known as Woodside. In the early 1930s, unhappy with California's tax

Whittell's African Lion cub, Bill, accompanied him most everywhere, often riding in the front seat of his Dusenberg.

laws, Whittell decided to become a Nevada resident. When a real estate deal Whittell had backed went wrong, he suddenly became the sole owner of nearly 25,000 acres of the Lake Tahoe Basin including twenty-seven miles of lakefront. His holdings encompassed essentially 95% of the Nevada shore-line of Lake Tahoe. He soon purchased additional land, eventually growing his Lake Tahoe holdings to nearly 45,000 acres.

In 1935, Whittell began work on a lakefront residence which he named Thunderbird Lodge. Hiring renowned architect Frederic DeLongchamps from Reno for the design, Whittell's stone house and ancillary buildings were constructed over the next few years. The main house had no guest rooms, as Whittell did not want any overnight guests.

One of the main features of Whittell's Thunderbird Lodge is the beautiful rock work found throughout the estate. The nearby Stewart Indian School in Carson City had a stone mason vocational program for the young Native American men. Whittell hired dozens of them to help construct stonework for the elaborate walkways, home, and other structures now at Thunderbird Lodge.

The estate included a card house, caretaker's cottage, a residence for the help, an Admiral's House, a boathouse with an adjoining 600-foot tunnel leading to the main house, a gatehouse, and the "Elephant House"—home to Mingo, Whittell's two-ton pet elephant who was only at his Lake Tahoe's estate for a short time. The large boathouse housed his custom 55-foot-long mahogany and stainless-steel yacht, the *Thunderbird*.

Early on, Whittell had plans for a few major developments on his Lake Tahoe property, including casinos at Zephyr Cove and Sand Harbor. But as the years passed, he grew more reclusive and favored his privacy at his secluded hideaway. All plans for commercial development of his property faded. He continued to entertain friends including neighbor and former baseball great and part time Tahoe resident Ty Cobb, fellow eccentric recluse Howard Hughes, and other Lake Tahoe area friends and acquaintances who enjoyed the high stakes games.

In addition to Mingo the elephant, Whittell began to amass a large animal collection, some brought back with him from African adventures, including tigers, a giraffe, a bear, and many more. A lion cub named Bill was one of Whittell's favorite companions, and it often rode along with him in the front seat of one of his luxury cars. A car collector, who had later bought one of Whittell's classic Duesenbergs, recalls, "It had scratches on the seat. He used to let this 300-pound lion sit shotgun with him, and its claws would come out and put holes in the seat."

He referred to his three aircraft as the "Whittell Air-force." There was a DC-2 that served as his domestic, luxury aircraft in which he flew friends to boxing matches and other social events across the country. He had an amphibious airplane, the Grumman Goose, that he used to fly between the Bay Area and his Lake Tahoe home, and he sold his interest in his 307 Stratoliner to Howard Hughes, before it was even completed.

But without a doubt, his pride and joy was his yacht, the *Thunderbird*, a 55-foot, mahogany and stainless-steel, twin-V12-powered marvel. Designed by famed boat architect John L. Hacker, it was built by Huskins Boat Works in Bay City, Michigan at a cost of $87,000—about $1.8 million today. The boat is a one-off streamline modern masterpiece, and has been said it looked like a burnished, wooden, floating Miami Beach hotel.

In the early 1950s, Whittell hired a young attorney, Paul Laxalt, who would go on to become Governor of Nevada in 1966. Laxalt advised Whittell to donate some of his land to non-profit organizations including University Nevada Reno, St. Mary's Hospital, and Douglas County for construction of a new high school (now George Whittell High School). In 1958, Whittell leased nine acres of Lake Tahoe waterfront (Sand Harbor) to the State of Nevada for a state park. Six years later, he was forced by court order to sell an additional 5,300 acres to Nevada, which became Lake Tahoe Nevada State Park, now host to one million visitors a year.

In 1959, Whittell sold nine thousand acres for $5 million to a group of investors, who turned around the very next year and sold the land to the Crystal Bay Development Company for a 500 percent profit. The developers subdivided the property into 1,700 lots, which ultimately became the town of Incline Village, located near the Incline tramline that was used to transport lumber during the heyday of Virginia City and the Comstock Lode (see chapter 23). Today, Incline Village has a population of over 9,000 residents, making it the second largest community in the Lake Tahoe Basin.

By the mid-1950s, Whittell's health began to decline, and he spent less and less time at his Lake Tahoe estate. He passed away in 1969 with his second wife Elia by his side. He made provisions in his will for Elia, as well as his longtime nurse and caregiver. The remainder of his estate, he divided between the Audubon Society, the Defenders of Wildlife, and the Society for the Prevention of Cruelty to Animals.

Most of Whittell's property was bought by Wall Street investor Jack Dreyfuss. Over the next few years, through a complex series of land exchanges and purchases, the remainder of his property was obtained by the U.S. Forest Service and Nevada State Parks System, and is now public lands for people to enjoy today. Thunderbird Lodge has come under the stewardship of the non-profit Thunderbird Lodge Preservation Society which does a masterful job in maintaining the home and adjoining property. They also offer fascinating tours of the estate in the summer months: For more information, https://thunderbirdtahoe.org/

Unconventional Lake Tahoe resident George Whittell Jr.'s decision to not pursue development of the 27-miles of shoreline he owned was more from his desire for privacy and seclusion, rather than intentional conservation. But, because of this "twist of fate," we can indisputably thank the good Captain for the natural and unspoiled beauty of most of Lake Tahoe's present-day northeastern shoreline.

George Whittell built his Thunderbird Lodge on Lake Tahoe's waterfront a few miles south of Sand Harbor. Tours are available in the summer from https://thunderbirdtahoe.org/

Tales Along
LAKE TAHOE SHORES

CHAPTER THIRTEEN

LIFE CAN BE A WILD RIDE

Log Fluming at Lake Tahoe

It has been said that the success and enormous profits of the great Comstock Lode of Virginia City would not have been possible without the forests of Lake Tahoe. The huge trees provided lumber to support the hundreds of miles of tunnels dug in search of silver and gold. Wood was also used as fuel for the stamp mills and to build homes and businesses for the town's 30,000 residents. And correspondingly, the forests of Lake Tahoe would never have been able to fulfill the lumber needs of the Comstock, if it weren't for the invention of the infamous V-flume. Though horses, mules, and small logging railroads were all used to move wood at Tahoe, it was the V-flume that revolutionized its lumbering.

The V-flume is nothing more than a giant trough of 2-inch-thick woodplanks, 2-feet wide and 16-feet long, nailed together into a V. They were occasionally lined with metal sheathing. A constant source of water was needed to run down the flume, which carried the wood downhill to a landing.

Lumberman J.W. Haines from Douglas County, NV is given credit for devising this extremely efficient method of transport in 1859. The first flume was built from Hunter Creek on the slopes of Mt. Rose to a Virginia and Truckee Railroad station in the Washoe Valley. The flume contained 2-million board feet of lumber and 28 tons of spikes and nails. It operated 70-feet above ground in some places and could transport up to a half-million board feet of lumber daily. Employing 200 men, the flume's builders completed the 15 miles of wood conduit in just 10 short weeks at a cost of $250,000. The new contrivance worked so well, log flumes spread throughout the forests of the western United States, as "man-made rivers" brought lumber to market.

It was claimed the flume did the work of 2,000 horses, and quickly became to many a "wooden wonder of the West." It sparked the curiosity and interest of people far and wide.

In the summer of 1875, H.J. Ramsdell, a reporter for the *New York Tribune*, had heard tales of Nevada's great flumes and decided to see one for himself. James Fair and J.C. Flood were both principals in the company that built one of what now were several Tahoe area V-flumes, and invited Ramsdell to see their "Eighth Wonder of the World" up close.

Ramsdell was thoroughly impressed by the Comstock men's ingenuity. What happened next is left to conjecture, but in short order, arrangements were being made for Ramsdell, Flood, and Fair to "ride the flume" from beginning to end to measure its efficiency. John Hereford, who oversaw the construction and operation of the flume, was drawn into their hair brain scheme.

Log flume owners James Fair (L) and J.C. Flood (R).

Flume workers hurriedly constructed two V-shaped "boats", which were simply a smaller and narrower version of the flume itself. The contraptions were christened "hog troughs" by the men who built them. The fronts were left open, and the rear portions were closed with boards, against which the water would push the boats forward.

Fair told Ramsdell he would ride with him in the lead boat. But as the start of their harrowing descent approached, Fair instructed one of the workers who was familiar with the flume's route to accompany them for "safety and advice." Flood and Hereford would be in the second boat…which with two men instead of three, seemed to be destined to eventually overtake the heavier, lead vessel while they descended.

V-flumes were easy to construct and became the most efficient method to transport wood down from the high mountains.

As soon as the men got into the "troughs," they rocketed down the flume like missiles. The hastily built boats lurched and pitched wildly down the

48

curving water filled course. The flume spanned deep gullies on sky high trestles and clung precariously to near vertical cliffs. The occupants would later admit they divided their time between cursing their stupidity and making peace with their maker.

When composure was regained, the men reflected on their ordeal. James Flood stated that he would never make this trip again, even for all the value of his mine holdings. The trembling Flume superintendent Hereford said he was sorry he ever built the flume. As for newspaperman H.J. Ramsdell, his feelings were very clear. "For myself," he wrote, "I had only strength enough to say… I have had enough of flumes."

Several V-flumes were built in the Lake Tahoe area. There are still pieces of aging, cracked wood lying in the canyons that were once used by the flumes. When Tahoe lumbering stopped at the turn of the century, this once-vital piece of ingenuity was left rotting and abandoned but not quite forgotten. This simple, but well thought out and designed, device illustrates the brilliance and creative skill of the 19th century Americans.

If it's true that there are no atheists in foxholes, then so it's true that the five men riding the flume that day in 1875, were as devout as they ever would be. Ramsdell returned to the *New York Tribune* to report to his readers that something of substance did indeed exist outside the haute environs of the eastern seaboard.

Huge trestles supported the V-flumes as they would cross canyons and draws... sometimes 100' or more above grade.

Loggers would sometimes ride the flumes down the mountains and out of the woods to get a faster start on their days off.

Tales Along
LAKE TAHOE SHORES

CHAPTER FOURTEEN
A LASTING PART
OF HISTORY
The Osgood Tollhouse

Winters in the High Sierra are cold and snowy…summers are filled with desiccating dry air and intense sunlight. These extremes can be hard on man and beast, and can also take their "toll" on old structures. There aren't many buildings that have stood for long in the Lake Tahoe area, but the oldest and one of the most historic pieces of Tahoe area architecture sits proudly and appropriately at the Lake Tahoe Historical Society Museum in South Lake Tahoe.

Osgood's Toll House was originally built in 1859 by Nehemiah Osgood. Osgood was a smart businessman who came west from New Hampshire to the Lake Tahoe area in the late 1850s. He noticed the large volume of traffic moving to and from the great Comstock Lode of Virginia City over Johnson's Pass (now Echo Summit) and thought there must be a financial opportunity there.

Nehemiah obtained a small parcel of land at the eastern foot of the grade adjacent to Echo Creek in what we know today as Meyers. He constructed a small cabin for his business, as well as another building nearby to live in. He told travelers he maintained the road in that area and charged five cents per animal and $1.50 for men and their wagons to pass in either direction.

In the 1860s and '70s, the state was not in the road building or maintenance business, and entrepreneurs sprouted up everywhere to fill in the void, and build and maintain wagon roads. There were several toll houses in the Lake Tahoe area, each with an operator who would collect tolls and keep their section of road maintained and in good condition.

Business was good for Nehemiah and his operation grew. Within a few years he employed at least three toll keepers to help handle the traffic. The completion of the Transcontinental Railroad in 1869 made crossing the Sierra Nevada Mountains infinitely easier, and traffic across Johnson's Pass took a steep decline. Osgood eventually closed his toll house, and the building stood empty for three decades, like a sorrowful monument to a more prosperous time.

In 1911, a large spring runoff burst the small dam at Echo Lake (see chapter nine), and a flood of water cascaded down Echo Creek and washed Osgood's old toll house off its foundation.

Still basically intact, Lake Tahoe pioneer family, the Celios, rescued Osgood's old building and moved it to their nearby property close to Yank's Station. The Celios kept the historic structure from deteriorating further, and it stood on their property for the next 50 years.

In the 1960s, a group of investors named the Tahoe Paradise Corporation came into the picture and started plans to develop 4,500 acres in the area. Osgood's Toll House was moved out of the way to the edge of the Tahoe Paradise Golf Course, where it remained until May of 1974.

Without the caretaking of the Celios, the historic building began to fall into disrepair, but thankfully caught the attention of the newly formed (1968) Lake Tahoe Historical Society/Museum. The history minded folks arranged to have the Toll House moved into South Lake Tahoe, and later moved one final time to its current location at the Lake Tahoe Museum, 3058 Lake Tahoe Blvd., South Lake Tahoe, California. The oldest standing commercial building in the South Lake Tahoe area is currently (2023) being renovated and restored. When the Museum's work is completed, it will be open to the public to enjoy.

The Lake Tahoe Historical Society Museum is a "must see" for anyone who enjoys history. It features displays and artifacts which chronicle the development of the Lake Tahoe Basin including: the earliest inhabitants – the Washo, John Fremont's "discovery" of Lake Tahoe, westward moving wagon trains, gold and silver rush traffic through the Basin, Pony Express stations, the logging and railroad industries, early steamships, and the development of tourism, skiing, and gaming. One of the largest exhibits is part of the old dairy operated by the Celio family who first settled in the Lake Tahoe area in 1857.

In addition to the exhibits inside, directly behind the museum is the Old Log Cabin built in 1931, one of Tahoe's oldest private residences. And a few blocks away at the Bijou Community Park is the Museum's Lake Valley Railroad narrow gauge and log carrier exhibit.

For more information on the Lake Tahoe Historical Society and Museum, visit their webpage: http://www.laketahoemuseum.org/home.html

The Osgood Toll House is the oldest existing building in the Lake Tahoe area, and now is located at the Lake Tahoe Museum- South Lake Tahoe.

CHAPTER FIFTEEN
THE BIG BANG
The 1980
Harvey's Casino Bombing

Tales Along
LAKE TAHOE SHORES

Janos (John) Birges Sr. was born in Hungary in 1922. He claimed to have flown with the German Luftwaffe (Hungary was an ally of Germany for much of World War II), and later fought with the Hungarian resistance against Soviet forces when they occupied his native country. He was captured by the Soviets and sentenced to 25 years of hard labor in Siberia and released after 8 ½ years. Birges married his wife Elizabeth, immigrated to the United States and settled in Fresno, California. They both got work on a farm, John as a carpenter and Elizabeth in the packing house. A few months later, John found work with a metal-fabrication company, PDM Steel. He spent five years there, where he honed his skills at welding and pipefitting. They had two sons, John Jr. (Johnny) and James (Jimmy).

John Sr. started his own landscaping outfit. He worked hard, rarely taking days off and became very successful. Over the years, some of his work brought him to blasting wells and trenches out of the California hardpan, and John became quite experienced at using dynamite.

By 1972, Big John was a millionaire, with three separate businesses, 26 employees, and lucrative contracts with California municipalities and golf courses. He bought three Mercedes Benz and his own airplane that he used to fly to job sites. John and Elizabeth opened a restaurant in Fresno called the Villa Basque, which was an immediate hit. No matter his wealth and success, John always retained an interest in tinkering and developed several gizmos and contraptions out of his large workshop.

But all was not perfect. John and Elizabeth drank heavily and fought often. They divorced, and, in 1975, Elizabeth overdosed on a combination of alcohol and Valium, and died. John changed after her death. He began spending money like never before, including at the 21 tables at Harvey's Wagon Wheel at Lake Tahoe, Nevada. John became known as a high roller at Harvey's. His rooms were always comped, he was invited to hunt pheasant on the casino's private ranch, he was flown around in Harvey's private helicopter...and he gambled (and mostly lost) hundreds of thousands of dollars.

By the late 1970s, John's propensity for gambling huge sums began to take its toll. Harvey's began sending their debt collector to John's Fresno home for checks that he had bounced. He wrote another $15,000 of NSF checks, and then his fabled restaurant burned to the ground. John collected $300,000 in insurance...and lost all of it at blackjack. Harvey's had comped his suite for New Year's Eve 1979, but in an ego shattering incident, John was told a few hours later he had to vacate it for another casino player and

53

move to a "standard" room. At the end of the decade, John Birges Sr. was broke and humiliated. Despondent, depressed, out of money and seething with revenge, John began to formulate a plan to get even and get the money he had gambled away…back.

It was about 5:30 a.m. on Tuesday, August 26, 1980, when Bob Vinson, who supervised the graveyard shift at Harvey's, realized he was out of cigarettes. He was on his way down from his second-floor casino office to the gift shop to buy a pack when he noticed something odd. There was a large gray metal box sitting there, right outside the phone exchange room.

Thirty minutes earlier, 24-year old Terry Hall and 59-year old Bill Brown had pushed the heavy metal box, draped with a covering tarp that said "IBM," through the front doors of the casino to a service elevator. No one seemed to notice, much less question, the two men and their heavy cart as they passed through the gambling house. John Birges Sr. met Hall and Brown in a parking lot outside the casino, after they had placed their load by the casino's second-floor offices.

Bob Vinson immediately called casino security. A Douglas County deputy sheriff soon arrived. An envelope was seen on the carpet next to the suspicious metal box. They poked at the envelope with a janitor's broom and dragged it to them. Inside were three neatly typed pages.

"Stern warning to the management and bomb squad," the note began. *"Do not move or tilt this bomb, because the mechanism controlling the detonators will set it off at a movement of less than .01 on the open end Richter scale. Don't try to flood or gas the bomb. There is a float switch and an atmospheric pressure switch set at 26.00-33.00. Both are attached to detonators. Do not try to take it apart. The flathead screws are also attached to triggers… WARNING: I repeat do not try to move, disarm, or enter the bomb. It will explode."*

The letter went on to claim the bomb was filled with 1,000 pounds of TNT, enough to not just obliterate Harvey's but also severely damage Harrah's Casino across the street. It was equipped with three separate timers. The letter advised cordoning off a minimum of 1,200 feet around the building and evacuating the area. "This bomb can never be dismantled or disarmed without causing an explosion," it said. "Not even by the creator."

The letter's author was demanding $3 million in used $100 bills, delivered by helicopter to intermediaries, with further details to follow. In exchange, instructions would be provided for how to disconnect two of the automatic timers so the device could be moved to a location where it would explode harmlessly. Once the ransom was paid, five sets of the instructions would be sent by general delivery to the Kingsbury Post Office in Stateline. There was a tight deadline: "There will be no extension or renegotiation. The transaction has to take place within 24 hours." The note concluded with a message for the helicopter pilot making the ransom drop. "We don't want any trouble, but we won't run away if you bring it," it said. "Happy landing."

Harvey's Casino was immediately evacuated. Guests in their bed clothes huddled in the parking lot waiting to be transported to safe locations. Casino chips and cash laid abandoned on the craps and twenty-one tables. Breakfast in the steam-tables at the buffet began to congeal.

54

FBI bomb experts arrived on the scene and assumed command of the situation. X-rays taken of the box showed there were indeed 28 toggle switches connected to screws, triggers, a collapsing circuit, and pressure release switches. The dynamite was packed in so tightly the portable X-ray machine couldn't penetrate it. The G-men came to the conclusion they were looking at the largest improvised bomb in U.S. history.

Nevada Fire Marshal Tom Huddleston inspects the bomb placed at Harvey's Casino.
A command post was set up. Officers were sent out to locate witnesses. The National Guard and local sheriffs set up a perimeter, and people were evacuated. The FBI sent more agents. Within two hours, word of the bomb has spread throughout the country. News trucks from Reno set up in the Sahara (now Hard Rock) parking lot next door. Scientists from three different

federal agencies arrived to assist.

The FBI determined the bomb could not be moved and that the safest thing was to try and disarm the bomb where it stood, and an explosion inside the casino...was highly likely. When told this, Harvey's owner Harvey Gross made his decision. "There's no way I'm paying these sons of bitches any money."

John Birges Sr. drove back to Fresno to await the "next steps." He had enlisted his two sons to help with the ransom pay off. The convoluted plan was laid out:

- Son Johnny would drop off his father and brother Jimmy at a clearing near Ice House Reservoir off Hwy. 50, 30-miles west of Lake Tahoe, with guns and a strobe light.
- A helicopter with the ransom money would be instructed to fly in their general direction following Hwy. 50. When the helicopter neared the pair, the strobe light would be flashed and the pilot was to land.
- When the helicopter was on the ground, the pilot would be overpowered, and John Sr. would fly the chopper to a second clearing, 40-miles south near Hams Station on Hwy. 88, where Johnny would be waiting in the car.
- Jimmy and the money would go with Johnny, while John Sr. flew the helicopter to Cameron Park twenty miles west of Placerville, where his girlfriend Joan would be waiting in a car to whisk him away.
- The four would then rendezvous back in Fresno.

Things went south from the very start:

- The battery to power the strobe light was forgotten. The trio first tried to steal one from a car parked at a closed gas station (Fresh Pond?). Barking dogs and an angry owner chased them off. They had to drive 30 miles back to a 24-hour gas station in Placerville to purchase a battery.
- Johnny called the FBI to tell them of the drop off instructions. But his less than clear orders and John Sr.'s delay caused the helicopter pilot to miss his mark in the dark, and never see John Sr.'s strobe light.
- After five hours of waiting in the dark, Johnny finally thought something must have gone wrong, and drove back to the Ice House Road to find John Sr. and Jimmy. Johnny first stopped at Cameron Park and told John's girlfriend Joan to follow him back to Ice House in her car.
- On the way, Johnny watched in horror as he saw Joan slide off Hwy. 50 in his rearview mirror. The car was wrecked; Joan was bleeding from her nose and head. She got into Johnny's car, and they continued towards John Sr. on Ice House Rd. They found John and Jimmy about 6:00 a.m. on Wednesday August 27.
- With the ransom drop failed, they drove Joan to Placerville and dropped her off at a hospital. The three men went to a pay phone where John called the FBI. He told them to switch toggle "five" on the bomb, which would delay an explosion, and await further instructions.

Back at Lake Tahoe, the FBI and bomb experts decided to attempt a procedure they hoped would disarm the bomb. A small charge was attached to the bomb in a specific spot. The hope was this small detonation would "decapitate" the trigger switch before it had an opportunity to ignite the entire bomb. At 3:30 p.m. gawkers and onlookers were told to move further back from Harvey's. At 3:46 p.m., the FBI detonated the small charge…which was followed immediately by a thunderous roar. Birges' bomb had exploded.

Fragments of concrete, glass, and plaster rained from the sky. Bits of wood, metal, and glass sprayed out both sides of the casino. The massive bomb sent out a pressure wave upward at 1,400 feet per second, blasting a massive crater up through five floors of the casino/hotel.

John Sr. heard the news of the blast on the radio while heading back to Placerville to pick up Joan from the hospital. It is said he told his son Jimmy, "Well, I don't have anything to live for now."

Government bomb experts swarmed upon the scene to collect evidence, but it was sparse in coming. Harvey Gross announced a $200,000 reward assembled by the four Stateline casinos for information leading to the arrest of the perpetrator(s).

One lead led them to a South Lake Tahoe motel John, Terry Hall, and Bill Brown had stayed at the night before they had placed the bomb. But they had registered under a phony name and address, and the trail dead ended.

Within 10-days, the FBI had five suspects they felt confident were the culprits. But after intense interviewing, the agents realized they did not have their men. The FBI investigation remained intense. The IRA, Iranian students, and the Mafia were all considered as possible suspects. Hundreds of leads and tips were investigated, but nothing solid turned up. That was, until October. Good detective work helped lead the FBI to Johnny Birges through the white van used to deliver the bomb, and identified by the motel owner where they stayed. The van was registered to Johnny. John helped Johnny concoct an elaborate story as to why the van was at Lake Tahoe the night before the bomb was placed. When he finished his explanation, the agents told him his story was ridiculous and unbelievable. Johnny was added to the FBI's list of suspects, but nothing more happened for the time being.

The FBI interviewed John Sr. but came up with nothing they felt could lead to an arrest. Months continued to pass. One group of investigators was trying to track down a former Harvey's employee who reportedly held a grudge against his former employer. But still no prime suspects were arrested.

In May of 1981, just nine months after the bombing and $18-million in repairs later, Harvey's Wagon Wheel Casino reopened for business. The reward to find those that had placed the bomb had grown to $500,000.

Around this same time, "the" lead came in. A man called in saying he had dated a woman, who had told him she was the former girlfriend of Johnny Birges, and that Johnny had told her of his involvement in the bombing. The FBI wired the young man, confirmed the girl's story, and ramped up their investigation of John Sr. Their relentless investigative efforts led to several clues that indicated it "could" be John, but nothing iron clad. Finally, under intense questioning by a grand jury, Jimmy and Johnny Birges crumbled and confessed everything.

Bill Brown and Terry Hall were convicted and sentenced to seven years each. John Sr. was convicted in federal and state courts and sentenced to twenty-years. Due to their cooperation with the FBI, Johnny and Jimmy received a sentence of three years felony probation.

John Sr. died in prison of liver cancer in 1996. Though his plan to collect the ransom money was straight out of a Keystone Cops scene, his ingenuity

Tahoe Daily Tribune

Serving All Lake Tahoe
America's
All-Year Playground

VOL. 22. NO. 191   541-3880   SOUTH LAKE TAHOE, CALIFORNIA   TUESDAY, AUGUST 26, 1980   3 SECTIONS — 40 PAGES   PRICE 25 CENTS

BOMB CLOSES CASINO

Tuesday

Lake Tahoe

THEIR RUINS not only provide the free clinics with a good time for themselves, but also benefit charity organizations. They're the Clown Patrol, who marked out at the Special Olympics at Heavenly Valley.

Page 11

The World

POLISH STRIKERS resumed negotiations today after the Communist regime restored telephone communications.

A massive bomb was discovered this morning in the executive offices of Harvey's Resort Hotel, resulting in evacuation of hundreds of persons and closure of the high-rise Stateline hotel-casino.

The apparent extortion attempt and evacuation brought Highway 50 traffic almost to a standstill. Automobiles backed up for miles into California, and some traffic was re-routed over the Loop Road.

Most South Shore law enforcement and firefighting personnel were called in to assist Douglas County authorities, and Barton Memorial Hospital asked nursing personnel to stand by in case the bomb exploded.

Douglas County Sheriff Jerry Maple refused to comment on the case this morning, other than to say deputies and firemen were investigating.

Maple even refused to confirm the presence of a bomb in the hotel. Hotel

The Harvey's bombing drew worldwide attention.

building and placing the bomb was remarkable. FBI bomb experts used a prototype of Birges' bomb for several years to conduct explosives training.

It can be said that much "good" stemmed from the Harvey's Wagon Wheel bombing. The incident brought increased and heightened security throughout the country and initiated new methods to thwart such attempts in the future. But the Harvey's bombing remains a sad and discordant page in the many history tales of Lake Tahoe.

The bomb was detonated when the FBI attempted to disarm it. The blast blew through five floors of the hotel and rained debris for hundreds of feet.

CHAPTER SIXTEEN
A MAN OF MANY FACES
Duane L. Bliss

Duane L. Bliss came to the famous Comstock of Western Nevada in the early 1860s. Bliss made many good connections and quickly became the superintendent of one of the first quartz mills at Virginia City. He then opened one of the area's first banks, and soon merged with the powerful "Bank Ring," a group of wealthy Bay Area men, who soon controlled most of the mining shares on the Comstock.

The pine forests on the east slope of the Sierra Nevada were quickly harvested to provide needed fuel and timbers as Virginia City's silver mining grew. Needing a new source of wood, attention was focused on the Lake Tahoe Basin's "unlimited" forests. Bliss was convinced by his business partners to lead the Lake Tahoe wood cutting efforts. Bliss bought up tens of thousands of acres of Tahoe's magnificent forests. Trees were cut near Tahoe's shore, dropped into the lake, and rafted to Glenbrook where Bliss had built a few lumber mills.

Bliss had an eleven-mile log flume built from Spooner Summit to the south end of Carson City, where a huge lumber yard was built. Another flume was built to bring water from Marlette Lake (4.5 miles distant and 1,000' higher) to provide water for the flume. A narrow-gauge railroad hauled the lumber 800-feet up from the Glenbrook mills to the log flume at Spooner Summit. Another narrow-gauge railroad was built at South Lake Tahoe, to bring out the valuable timber to the lake shore's log rafts.

For 20 years, D.L. Bliss was king of the Tahoe lumber barons. At its peak, his logging operation would run round the clock. But, by the1890s, the great silver boom was in steep decline, and the demand for Tahoe's trees slowed to a trickle.

Bliss had already made his fortune and was on solid financial ground. He was also a visionary. He was looking for new opportunities as the demand for lumber decreased. Even with the Basin mostly denuded of trees, Lake Tahoe was still a beautiful scene. Bliss felt people would come to the Lake for pleasure and recreation if proper lodging and accommodations were available and travel made easier.

Bliss built a hotel at Glenbrook and acquired a steamship he dubbed the *S.S. Tahoe*. Tourists would take the train to Truckee, then the stage to Tahoe City, and board the *S.S. Tahoe* for a cross lake trip to his lodging at Glenbrook.

He also set in motion construction of a 225-room luxury hotel near Tahoe City he christened the Tahoe Tavern. When it opened in 1901, it was said to

Glenbrook was the hub of D.L. Bliss' Lake Tahoe lumber empire. The location supported three mills and a narrow gauge railroad to haul the wood products to the top of Spooner Summit for fluming. Note the logged off hillsides in the background. It was also the site of Bliss' first venture into tourism.

be the finest hotel between San Francisco and Denver. It had steam heat, running water, and electric lights. For those that needed to do business or stay in touch, Western Union Telegraph line, and later…a phone line was built. Can you imagine? Visiting a place as beautiful as Lake Tahoe…and feeling you had to stay "connected" with the outside world. Perhaps someday we'll learn our lesson!

The Lake Tahoe Railroad's passenger train would bring guests from Truckee to Tahoe City. The train would run right out onto the Lake on a pier, parallel to Bliss' passenger ship, which transported guests to his resort at Glenbrook.

D.L. Bliss had the upscale Glenbrook Inn built in 1907.
The Bliss family operated it until 1976.

Bliss had his Glenbrook and South Shore logging operations dismantled, loaded the locomotives and track onto barges, and brought them to Tahoe City. He had a railroad grade constructed from Tahoe City to Truckee, laid down the track, bought a few passenger cars, and opened the Lake Tahoe Railway, which connected the Southern Pacific RR main line at Truckee with Tahoe City. Tracks were even laid down on a pier that was extended hundreds of feet into Lake Tahoe, so patrons would only have to walk a few feet from the train to the passenger ship. Guests could now easily get to Bliss' resorts, and tourism in Lake Tahoe was off and running.

D.L. Bliss State Park on Lake Tahoe's west shore, was donated to the State by the Bliss family and is now one of the crown jewels of the California State Park system.

In 1929, the Bliss family donated 744 acres (including six miles of Lake Tahoe waterfront) to the State of California for a state park. Today, D.L. Bliss State Park is one of the crown jewels of the California State Park system, and a magnificent spot for all to enjoy.

Duane L. Bliss was one of the most successful businessmen to have ever called Lake Tahoe home. His business ventures included mining, logging, transportation, and hospitality.

Tales Along
LAKE TAHOE SHORES

CHAPTER SEVENTEEN
WATER FOR
THE COMSTOCK
Marlette Lake

A tale was often repeated during the early days around Virginia City and Carson City. It was said, "the wastes of Washoe were so barren that wild animals, including the formidable grizzly bear, gazed eastward from the heights of the Sierra Nevada, sniffed the acrid air and quickly turned west back into the sanctuary of Tahoe's well-watered forests."

Folk lore or not, it is quite true that the land east of the Sierra crest averages a fraction of the precipitation received in the mountains just a few miles to the west.

The discovery of gold and silver at the Comstock Lode in 1859 set forth one of the greatest boom towns the U.S. has ever seen. By the 1870s, the population of Virginia City and the surrounding towns was estimated to be over 25,000 inhabitants. The town already had a reputation for being a thirsty place, but it was parched with another thirst that all the whiskey in the West could not quench.

The valuable silver and gold had to be extracted from the ore taken from the ground. The complicated process required millions of gallons of water each day. The good citizens of Virginia City needed water to cook, and though hard to believe, the miners were also known to take an occasional bath as well as a drink of water.

At first, the few springs on the arid slopes of the Virginia Range supported the townspeople and the mining, but as the town grew, it became quite evident a great deal more H2O would be required if the town were ever to reach its obvious potential.

In 1872, the Virginia and Gold Hill Water Company sent out engineer H. Schussler to find a new water source to solve their shortage of liquid gold. Schussler felt the water flowing from the east slope of the Sierra Nevada Mountains was just the right solution to the city's shortage.

Franktown (now known as Hobart) Creek lies a mere 12 miles as the crow flies from the bustling Virginia City metropolis. Its ample flow could significantly impact the town's water deficit. Just one major challenge…the water would have to be moved and "lifted" over 1,400-feet to get over the mountains to Virginia City.

Schussler already had a reputation as a very qualified engineer. He had designed the Spring Valley Water Works of San Francisco before the silver barons brought him to the Comstock. As a side note of interest…the two earthen dams Schussler had constructed for water storage above San Francisco easily withstood the great 1906 earthquake.

Schussler designed a system to include a diversion dam high up on

Hobart Creek. This high elevation reservoir would provide water for a box flume, pressure pipe, and inverted siphon. It was the most elaborate water system ever attempted up to that time. Wrought iron pipe would need to be constructed to withstand the tremendous pressure of the water dropping nearly 2,000 vertical feet before it began its 1,400' climb to Virginia City.

Brilliant Hermann Schussler designed the sophisticated water system from above Lake Tahoe, down the eastern slope, across the Washoe Valley and up to Virginia City.

Thirteen deep ravines or canyons would need to be crossed in the course of the new pipeline. Workers had a 30" trench dug by spring of 1873, and the first pipe was laid on June 11. By the 25th of July, in only seven short weeks, Schussler and his men had completed the mind-bending project.

Water was brought from the storage reservoir to the pipe inlet by a wooden box flume. The water coursed down the pipe and back up the Virginia Range by siphon. When it exited the pipe on the east side of the Virginia Mountain Range, the water would be carried the remaining seven miles in yet more flumes. The seven miles of 12" diameter steel pipe was constructed in 26' long sections, in thicknesses ranging from 1/16" to 5/16". The total pipe weighed an astounding 700 tons and was hauled to the site by the Virginia & Truckee (V&T) Railroad. There were 1,524 fitted joints secured by a like number of metal connector rings. Hundreds of thousands of rivets were used, and thirty-five tons of lead poured for caulking.

As the population of Virginia City grew, so did its need for more water.

When the water company opened the valves in Virginia City, a huge celebration began. Whistles at the mines and cannon fire from the militia announced to the world Virginia City had water. A torchlight parade passed through the city over and over till the break of dawn.

It is said there was only one flaw with the system. A pencil size hole on one section of the pipe grew to three inches in a matter of moments once the system was put under pressure. A jet of water spurted two hundred feet into the air from the hole. It was reported that the pressure of the escaping water was so great that it turned a man's fingernails down as though he had held them against a spinning emery wheel.

The increase in available water led of course to an increase in demand. Virginia City continued to grow, and, in less than three years, more water was needed than the new system could deliver. In 1876, a second pipe was laid parallel to the original system, significantly increasing available water for the Comstock. Over the next few years, the system was expanded even further, bringing water from higher up the mountain at Marlette Lake. The system still provides water for Virginia City (and Carson City) today.

Marlette Lake (center right) sits about 700 feet above Lake Tahoe (center lower) in the Carson Range near Sand Harbor.

The Virginia City/Marlette Lake water system was made up of pipe, troughs, and box flumes.

CHAPTER EIGHTEEN

Tales Along
LAKE TAHOE SHORES

SIERRA SUPERHERO
John "Snowshoe" Thompson

John "Snowshoe" Thompson is perhaps one of the most compelling and intriguing characters from not just the Lake Tahoe region, but in all of western history. His bravery and courage in carrying the U.S. Mail over the snow laden Sierra Nevada mountains during the winter months…for 20 years…is the kind of thing superhero tales are made from.

John was born in the Telemark region of Norway in 1827. This area is often credited with being the birthplace of cross-country skiing. The word ski comes from the Norwegian word 'skíð', which means "stick of wood." John was the youngest of 14 children. His father ranched and farmed, and cut and milled timber, enabling them to eke out a subsistence living. When Thompson was just two, an older brother, soon followed by his father, passed away.

Unable to keep the farm operating on her own, his mother moved into town and sought work as a domestic. Winters in Norway are long, cold, and snowy. The older members of Thompson's family used "snow-skates" to travel around during the frosty time of year. Snow-skates were very similar to what we know as cross-country skis today. It is thought Thompson himself used them in his adolescence.

Frustrated by her inability to feel like she was ever getting ahead, Thompson's mother scrimped and saved enough money to buy two tickets for passage to the United States. Leaving her other children with relatives and friends, she and John boarded a sailing ship to the United States in the spring of 1837. They settled in Illinois, and, for the next 13 years, John moved with his mother from Illinois to Missouri, Iowa, and Wisconsin. He developed skills in farming, ranching, and carpentry. By 1849, one of John's older brothers Thor had migrated from Norway and was living with him. That same year, the world learned that gold had been discovered in California. It seemed like everyone they knew was either making plans or talking about moving to California to claim their share of the "unlimited" yellow metal.

By the spring of 1851, John and Thor could take it no longer and began making their own plans to emigrate to California. They put together a small herd of dairy cows, thinking they could make money selling milk while searching for the gold, and joined a westward bound wagon train in the spring of 1851. Their trip west was fairly uneventful, and John settled in Hangtown (now Placerville) on the Sierra Nevada's western slope.

John immediately started searching for the gold he had read was so readily available. But like most of the gold seekers who came to California, quick riches evaded him. John gave it his best try, but soon gave up prospecting and rented agricultural land in the Central Valley west of Sacramento. Success at farming was as elusive as finding gold. Mother Nature was fickle, bringing drought, insects, and floods. John became discouraged with his decision to "move west."

In the winter of 1855, Thompson read an advertisement in the *Sacramento Union* newspaper. It stated that people of the east slope of the Sierra Nevada, Utah Territory (now Carson Valley, Nevada) lost all touch with the outside world during winter when deep snows cut off all communication. Uncle Sam was looking for someone who would carry the mail across the snow laden Sierra Nevada mountains during the winter.

John thought with his experience of winter travel gleaned from living in Norway and later Wisconsin, he would be just the right man to make the snowy trips. He obtained hardwood oak and cut it into two ten-foot lengths. He curved the tips up and crafted the boards six inches wide in the front, narrowing to four inches toward their ends. The boards were about 1/2" thick and at the middle of each, he attached a single leather strap under which he would place his boot. All together, they were said to weigh about 25 pounds. John made some of the first known skis in California and called them "snow skates."

He demonstrated his ability to move quickly (and almost effortlessly) across the snow to the Hangtown postmaster and was quickly hired to be the winter mail carrier. When he left for his first mail trip in January 1856, a great crowd had gathered in Hangtown to send him off. John hoisted the 80-pound sack of mail onto his shoulder and glided east. Someone in the excited crowd yelled out "Good luck Snowshoe Thompson"…and that became the common moniker he went by for the rest of his life.

John made the trip to Mormon Station (now known as Genoa) with ease. It took him three days to travel about 90-miles on his trip east, and only two days on the return westbound trip. He made the 180-mile round trip about twice a month for the remainder of that winter and resumed his route when the snows returned the next November.

Snowshoe Thompson carried the U.S. Mail over the Sierra Nevada during the winters for the next 20 years. His mail sack weighed as much as one hundred pounds. If he had room, he would carry other items patrons requested including the first ore samples of the famed Comstock Lode. He carried the first typeset for the new Virginia City newspaper, the *Territorial Enterprise,* where a young Mark Twain began his literary career.

To save weight (and carry more mail), he took no blanket or even a heavy coat. If caught in a severe storm, he would seek shelter under a rock overhang. If none were available, he would dance on a flat rock humming old Norwegian folk songs to keep the snow off and himself warm. He carried no gun, and only took food that did not require cooking. He was never lost and rarely took more than five days for the roundtrip.

Thompson experienced several situations that would challenge the toughest and bravest of men. He rescued several lost or snowbound people during his winter travels. In December of 1856, he worked all Christmas Day making snow skates and snowshoes so a rescue party he led the next day could bring out a near frozen James Sisson, marooned in a snow buried cabin in Lake Valley (now Meyers). After leading the rescue, he then made a marathon round trip to Sacramento from Genoa, to obtain chloroform so the physician could perform surgery on Sisson to remove his gangrene limbs.

On one of his trips, John encountered a pack of wolves as he entered the open expanse of Hope Valley. His route ahead would take him right near the wild animals. He put on his bravest face and skied within just a few yards of these infamous canines, fearing he would likely meet his mortal fate at any moment. As he passed at the closest point, the wolves let loose with a doleful and frightening howl that echoed across the hills. But no attack came, and John safely kept to his route.

John was hired as an Indian Agent for the Washo Tribe of Western Nevada in 1857. He did his best to provide the services the U.S. treaties had promised the Washo, but often felt frustrated the government did not live up to its promises to the Native Americans. After being forced to join the local militia in the Pyramid Lake Indian War of 1860, and nearly losing his life, he resigned his position.

Thompson was a man of his community. He eventually purchased land in Diamond Valley, California, just to the south of of Carson Valley, Nevada. He designed and dug by hand, two irrigation ditches over two miles long to bring water from the West Fork of the Carson River to his and his neighbor's farm lands. Farming during the summer when he was not carrying the mail…this time…John's attempts at farming succeeded.

He met and courted a neighbor's young housekeeper, Agnes Singleton, in 1866. John pursued her seriously and the two were soon married. Nine months later they brought Arthur Thompson into the world.

By now, prospectors had discovered a large silver deposit high in the Sierra Nevada Mountains southwest of Diamond Valley called Silver Mountain. John filed a mining claim on the snowbound peak and told Agnes he would work the claim between mail runs in the winter. Agnes told John she and Arthur would go with him to the new mine site. While high on Silver Mountain with very deep winter snows, young Arthur developed a fever and rasping cough. As Arthur's condition worsened, John told Agnes he would have to get them all off the mountain to the doctor in Genoa. He fashioned a crude harness around his waist and shoulders out of leather straps…had Agnes crawl onto his back…wrapped infant Arthur in every blanket they had…and carrying his son in his arms and his wife on his back, he skied the three of them off 6,500-foot Silver Mountain in deep winter snows. Thankfully, the Genoa doctor was able to return Arthur to health.

By 1869, John "Snowshoe" Thompson had carried the mail for the U.S. government for 13 years and as of yet, had never received direct compensation from the Postal Service for his work. He was allowed to collect any money people would pay him on the side, but most people expected him to carry their mail by simply affixing a stamp (five to ten cents). The reason most accepted by historians for this non-payment is that another man had been awarded a contract to carry the mail from Placerville to Salt Lake City in 1851, five years before Thompson began his route. The U.S. government expected the contractor to pay Thompson, but he never did. The contractor was often missing for weeks if not months at a time.

Despite this, Thompson dutifully carried the mail at least twice a month every winter across the Sierra Nevada. John felt it was his duty to make sure his neighbors received their mail, as hundreds of people counted on him to do so. John "Snowshoe" Thompson...never faltered.

John was the friend of all including a few Nevada State Legislators in Carson City. Learning of his "never been paid" situation with the U.S. government, a resolution was passed by the Nevada State Legislature in 1869, requesting the U.S. Government compensate Thompson for the 13 years he had carried the winter mail. The postmasters in Hangtown and Genoa signed on, as did dozens of others. But nothing came about...that was... until 1872.

In that year, John was told the U.S. Senate Committee on Post Offices, was going to take up a bill authorizing John be paid $6,000 for his now 16 years of mail carrying. The committee and then the full Senate passed the bill, but for reasons still unclear to this day, the House of Representatives never took up the bill, and John was never paid.

John continued his commitment to public service and the betterment of his fellow men and women. He served as an Alpine County Supervisor from 1868-1872. He ran for State Senator for Alpine County. He was always there to lend a hand to dig a ditch, erect a building, or bring in a harvest. He served his community unwaveringly.

In May of 1876, while planting that year's crop at his Diamond Valley farm, he experienced pulses of cold and hot. He grew fatigued and even had to ride his horse to finish the day's work. He quickly became bedridden... and soon passed away. At age 49, John "Snowshoe" Thompson's incredible life of bravery, courage, and commitment...came to an end. It is thought he fell victim to appendicitis which rapidly developed into pneumonia.

Today, John Thompson is honored by friends organizations, winter events, skiing competitions, statues, and plaques throughout the Lake Tahoe region and Western Nevada. But a hero is not merely a giant statue framed against a cloudless sky or a few words on a bronze plaque. It is a person that lives their life with care and concern for their community...their neighbors...their friends...and makes it their responsibility to make life better for all. And that indeed...was Snowshoe Thompson.

You can visit what is thought to be one of Snowshoe Thompson's shelter rocks just 3/4 mile east of Wylder Resort Hope Valley on California Highway 88. GPS coordinates 38.77867, -119.88744.

And though there are several different area museums that have displays/ information on Snowshoe Thompson, one of our personal favorites is the Lake Tahoe Museum, 3058 Lake Tahoe Blvd., South Lake Tahoe, California.

Snowshoe Thompson settled in Hangtown- now Placerville, when he moved west in 1851 for the California Gold Rush.

Snowshoe Thompson was a true super hero who called the Sierra Nevada home.

Snowshoe Thompson carried the mail throughout the Sierra Nevada Mountains. One route was along the west fork of the Carson River, now CA Hwy. 88.

This shelter rock on CA Hwy. 88, just east of Wylder Resort Hope Valley, is thought to have been used by Snowshoe Thompson.

Tales Along
LAKE TAHOE SHORES

CHAPTER NINETEEN
A PAINFUL LEGACY
The Stewart Indian School

Indian Schools in North America date back for hundreds of years. As early as the mid-1600s, Christian Missionaries obtained approval to start both missions and schools to "aid" the indigenous people. The primary objective was stated to be "civilizing" or assimilating Native American children and youth in Euro-American culture. Students were forbidden from speaking their native languages and were not allowed to engage in their traditional tribal practices. What resulted…was a denigrated Native American culture, where native languages, religions, and history were systemically erased. One of these Indian Schools was located just down the hill in Carson City, and shares a common thread of history with Lake Tahoe.

In 1889, Western Nevada was chosen by the U.S. Bureau of Indian Affairs as a location to build a new government Indian School. The lightly populated state found it difficult to provide an education for any of its residents, especially Native Americans living on remote rural lands.

Nevada Senator William Stewart sponsored the federal legislation that funded the Carson City school. Stewart Indian School opened on December 17, 1890. During the first 10 years, only children from the Nevada-based Washo, Paiute, and Western Shoshone tribes attended the school. Later, children from over sixty tribal groups including Hopi, Apache, Pima, Mohave, Walapai, Ute, Pipage, Coropah, and Tewa were forced to attend the school and leave their homes and families on these tribal reservations.

At first, the school depended on the unpaid labor of the students to help keep it open. They worked many hard hours washing clothes, cooking, farming, and performing other manual labor necessary to keep the school operating. After three years of such unfair practices, the students rebelled against their harsh treatment. Ultimately, Native American parents got the school to agree to give the children grades for their work and to be able to keep a portion of any money earned from their labor. By the 1930s, between 400 and 500 Native American students attended the Stewart School annually.

Native Americans were not given a choice to attend Indian schools. Children were forced to attend Stewart and other Indian schools up to secondary school age. In addition to eliminating the children's native language and culture, Stewart was also meant to provide Native youths with trade skills which would help to make them "fully American." Students during the early years were harshly disciplined. Some would escape and make their way back to their parents. If caught, they would be returned to the school. Stewart struggled in its mission, and the school went through a revolving door of superintendents. In 1919, Frederick Snyder was put in charge and implemented a real vocational program centered on architecture and horticulture.

A portion of Snyder's architecture program was centered around teaching the young men skills as stone masons. Using colored native stone quarried from along the Carson River, the male students were taught by Hopi stone-masons Snyder had brought from Arizona to help teach the Stewart youth. More than 60 buildings were built at Stewart by the Hopi and their students during this time.

In the mid 1930s, wealthy and eccentric George Whittell Jr. began making plans to build a summer home on his waterfront property a bit south of Sand Harbor, Nevada (see chapter 12). He hired famous Western Nevada architect Frederic DeLongchamps to design the buildings for his estate. The home and ancillary buildings would all be faced with native stone. Plans also called for hundreds of feet of stone walls and walkways. Whittell and De-Longchamps brought in students from Stewart's masonry program to do the work. Their detailed and beautiful efforts can be seen while on a tour of the Whittell Estate (https://thunderbirdtahoe.org/index.php/tours). The masonry work at Whittell's remains the largest off campus project undertaken by the Stewart Indian stone mason students.

In addition to its stone mason program, Stewart also taught its students skills in domestic service, carpentry, metal working, blacksmithing, harness making, cobbling, auto mechanics, and cattle ranching. Jacks Valley Ranch worked with the school providing a real-life ranching operation for students to learn and work in.

Policy in the Bureau of Indian Affairs slowly began to change around 1934, and the focus on assimilation by eradicating language and culture began to stop. Also in 1934, the Bureau of Indian Affairs placed at Stewart its first female school superintendent, Alida Bowler. Bowler believed in a curriculum that emphasized Native heritage and traditional crafts. She arranged public performances to familiarize non-natives with Native American culture, and encouraged the students to learn and express their traditional songs, dances, and art.

Bowler developed a reputation as a relentless advocate for Native American rights. Later, as an Indian Agent for almost the entire state of Nevada, she worked to help tribal councils get established and fought for their legal rights in the court system. She encouraged the Stewart youths to get involved in political issues as well. Bowler also worked hard to overcome racial prejudice in Nevada by desegregating schools in Elko in 1935 and Battle Mountain in 1936, and fought to desegregate schools in Lovelock, Smith Valley, and Yerington.

Over the years, Stewart developed a music program that became very popular and gained high recognition and accolades. The Stewart Band became the first Indian band to qualify for the National Regional Music Festival. Popular school band leader Earl Laird convinced the school to obtain band uniforms reflecting their Native American culture. Sharp looking sheepskin uniforms were fabricated by Paiute women at the Pyramid Lake Reservation.

By the 1960s, the mission of Federal Indian Schools had completely changed. Students were encouraged to speak and preserve their native languages and were taught their native cultures and traditions.

In 2021, young Native American Ku Stevens from Yerington, Nevada put together what he calls 'The Remembrance Run.' "The point of it all is to educate people on what happened to our people and what happened in Canada," said Stevens. "This is another way to recognize what kinds of things they did to be with their families." Steven's great-grandfather was a student at Stewart Indian School years before. When he was just 8-years old, he ran 50 miles to try and get back to his family on the Yerington Paiute tribal reservation. His route home went across the Nevada desert from Carson City to Yerington. He was caught and returned to Stewart, and escaped, again, three times in all.

Due to federal budget cuts and concern over earthquake safety, Stewart Indian School was closed in 1980. Today the former administration building at the school has been renovated into the new Stewart Indian School Cultural Center and Museum, thanks to funding from the Nevada State Legislature. The mission of the new Center is to tell the stories of the thousands of American Indian children from western tribes who were educated at Stewart. It is also a place of living heritage through exhibits of Native art, storytelling, arts and crafts demonstrations, and educational activities. The Stewart School site is also on the National Register of Historic Places.

The Cultural Center is open 10am-5pm Monday through Friday, and closed weekends and some holidays. For more information you can visit their website: https://stewartindianschool.com/museum/ or their address: 1 Jacobsen Wy., Carson City, NV 89701.

In its early years, the Stewart Indian School required all the Native youths to wear uniforms, cut their hair, speak only English, and learn all the ways of the white man's culture.

The stone masonry vocational program at Stewart was taught by Hopi Indians from Arizona. The Hopi and their Stewart School students built dozens of mostly stone structures on the Stewart Campus, many of which can be viewed today.

During its 90 years of existence, it is estimated over 30,000 Native American youths attended Stewart Indian School in Carson City.

CHAPTER TWENTY

Tales Along
LAKE TAHOE SHORES

CREATIVE WRITING
John Steinbeck at Lake Tahoe

Lake Tahoe has drawn creative souls to its tranquil and inspiring shores for millenniums. Washo peoples considered the lake sacred and the center of their world, providing abundant resources and spiritual fulfillment. A young John Muir wrote reverently of the Lake, "as if this {Tahoe} were a kind of water heaven to which all lakes had come." And legendary American author John Steinbeck was heartened and inspired by Lake Tahoe's essence, when he spent the better part of two years there after dropping out of Stanford University in the late 1920s.

Alternately, Steinbeck drove a bus for the Fallen Leaf Lodge, tutored the children of the original owners of Cascade Lake (Charles Brigham), and worked as what he referred to as a "piscatorial obstetrician" at the California State Fish Hatchery in Tahoe City.

Circa 1925, Mrs. William Wightman Price, the exacting proprietor of Fallen Leaf Lodge, came to the off-campus cottage of Steinbeck's near Stanford University. She demanded to know what endorsements he could provide to the character of a one, Toby Street. Street was Steinbeck's roommate and had recently proposed marriage to one of Price's female employees at Fallen Leaf. With the passion of a mother hen, Price had come to Palo Alto to investigate Street's moral character and potential as a husband.

The amused Steinbeck knew his hard drinking and fun-loving roommate as well as anyone. The two shared these passions with equal vigor as well as an interest in writing. But Steinbeck engaged his already well-honed creative skills and articulated the lamb-like and honorable traits of Street to Price so eloquently, she offered Steinbeck a position at her Lake Tahoe area resort.

Steinbeck quit Stanford and accepted Price's offer of employment. For the next two or three years (records are unclear), Steinbeck worked for Mrs. Price at Fallen Leaf Lodge shuttling tourists, and performing a myriad of maintenance duties. He supplemented this work with tutoring the children of the Charles Brigham family, and caretaking their Cascade Lake (between Baldwin Beach and Emerald Bay on Tahoe's southwest shore) estate in the winter, and shortly thereafter, the year around. Steinbeck became more than a caretaker to the Brighams, but a companion, hiking partner, and family friend as well. And when not carousing and reveling at what limited Lake Tahoe nightlife there was in those days, he found time to continue to develop his skills and talents as a writer.

In the late 1920s, most of Lake Tahoe was completely isolated during the winter months. It was during his winter isolation at Tahoe that Steinbeck completed his first published novel, *Cup of Gold*. He certainly put his "creative writing" talents to work during this time of his life, writing a bit "embellishing-ly," he had been "snowed in for eight months of the year at the Lake."

Before he left the Lake Tahoe area, Steinbeck spent some time working at the State Fish Hatchery in Tahoe City as a tour guide. It is thought it was here he met his first wife Carol Henning. After a whirlwind romance, the two married and moved to San Francisco, ending Steinbeck's time at Lake Tahoe.

At the height of his career Steinbeck said, "We find that after years of struggle, we do not take trips; a trip takes us…Many a trip continues long after movement in time and space have ceased." Perhaps it was the influence and reflection of his time at Lake Tahoe and the Sierra Nevada, that laid the foundation for this brilliant and skilled artist to become one of the finest literary talents of the 20th century.

John Steinbeck wrote his first novel while winter caretaking at Lake Tahoe.

Tales Along
LAKE TAHOE SHORES

CHAPTER TWENTY-ONE

WINTERS AT THE LAKE

Once the 1960 winter Olympics were held in Squaw Valley, winters at Lake Tahoe have been enjoyed by outdoor enthusiasts nearly as much as the summer months. With 15 ski resorts offering 560 miles of trails accessed by 177 ski lifts…and numerous cross-country ski and snow play areas intermingled around the Lake, winter sport devotees are not disappointed by booking a wintertime stay at Big Blue.

Winters in the Lake Tahoe Basin can be fickle. Mother Nature has a way of always delivering the unexpected. If you take the 50-year average for snowfall in the Sierra Nevada Mountains, 2 out of 3 years…are below average. Doing the math…when we have a "good" snow year at Lake Tahoe…its likely to be a "very good" snow year.

Many longtime Lake Tahoe residents and visitors have their own "I remember the winter of _____ . It snowed so much that (insert snow horror story here)_____." As recently as 2021, the Lake Tahoe area set the record for the most snow ever in the month of December…followed by the driest January and February ever. One winter that ingrained itself in the memories of all who experienced it was the winter of 1951-1952.

Storms began to bring snow to the Sierra Nevada before Halloween, and by New Year's Eve, 23 feet had fallen according to measurements at Donner Pass. On January 10, 1952, another storm king struck, and Donner Summit recorded 13 feet of new snow in just 7 days. If you didn't have a second story residence, you probably weren't able to exit your home. At the lakeshore, people dug tunnels to their second-floor windows so the sun would be able shine in.

Lake Tahoe was pretty remote in those days, and most winter residents were well prepared and stocked in advance with food, fuel, and firewood. The county and state highway departments had a very difficult time keeping the roads open, and many residents resorted to snowshoes and skis to get around. Those that had a difficult time were well cared for by others. Neighbors helping neighbors was the mantra that winter.

The first recorded sighting of Lake Tahoe by a Euro-American was made by Captain John C. Fremont in 1844. Fremont was almost out of food while on his second western expedition, and was struggling to make a winter crossing of the Sierra Nevada to obtain supplies at Sutter's Fort. On February 14, 1844, while scaling a high peak near current day Carson Pass, Fremont spotted in the distance "a great mountain lake." Fremont and his men had struggled through snow 21-feet deep. Fremont wrote in his journal, "…we

79

attempted in the afternoon to force a road through the deep drifts, but after a laborious plunging of two or three hundred yards our best horses gave out, entirely refusing to make any further effort."

Perhaps the most infamous of all Sierra Nevada winters was that which the forlorn Donner Party of 1846-1847 experienced. Early snows had blocked the Sierra Nevada pass by the end of October. Snow drifts over 25' soon buried their shelters back at Donner Lake, creating a desperate situation. Rescue parties were time and again turned back by raging storms. Even firewood could not be obtained as the trees were buried under snow. Tragically, over 40 pioneers lost their lives during that long and fateful winter.

In 1938, storm after storm pummeled the Lake Tahoe area. Roads were closed and communication was cut off for 21 days. Word got out that a horse had died at Glenbrook and that anyone that wanted meat for their dog to come get it. The story was picked up by a reporter for the *San Francisco Call Bulletin* and reprinted in other papers, that Tahoe residents were starving and were resorting to eating horse meat. Glenbrook resident Gene Viljoen recounted how shortly after the newspaper story appeared, a plane flew in low over Glenbrook and down came a bundle with a red streamer attached. Viljoen and others dug it out of six feet of snow and discovered 48 loaves of bread and 50 lbs. of meat. The arrival of fresh meat and bread was quite a treat and made the Glenbrook residents feel grateful for the concern and kindness of the people of San Francisco.

By the 1940s many visitors were trying to visit Lake Tahoe and Reno in the winter to enjoy outdoor sports. Resort owners Frank Globin (Globin's Resort in Al Tahoe) and Bill Harrah (Harrah's Club-Reno) lobbied the State Highway Department to keep the mountain highways open. The March 19, 1941 *San Francisco News* announced that Highways 40 and 50 were open to travelers and, "To celebrate the opening, resort owners have planned an elaborate program of activities centering at Curt Rocca's Echo Chalet."

Frosty winters in the mountains are as natural as the fragrance of pine on a warm summer day. It is quite possible to enjoy a frigid day on the snow as much as a warm July afternoon on Baldwin Beach. May we always enjoy the many different faces of beauty Mother Nature shows us.

"To appreciate the beauty of a snowflake it is necessary to stand out in the cold." Aristotle

A wintry Lake Tahoe scene. It may have taken awhile to dig this car and house out.

Up until the mid 1930s, drivers would have to dig the Sierra Nevada roads out by hand if they wished travel by auto in the winter.

ALL THE NEWS THAT'S FIT TO PRINT

Tahoe Daily Messenger: July 22, 1936
"With a feud race between Feishacker and Newhall as one of the highlights, a power boat race will held from Chamber's Resort Pier on August 9. These men have raced before and according to reports, in the last one Newhall was leading near the conclusion of the event when he ran out of gas. It is said he lost a considerable side bet to Fleishacker and is out to win it back in this upcoming race."

Tahoe Tattler: August,1881
"We are present having the most beautiful weather of the season. Neither too warm nor uncomfortably cool, but just right. Fishing never was better. Can't get any better meals on the coast than we have at the Tahoe hotels and there is no one on the Lake but who enjoy themselves. What more can we ask? The boss of this paper took a ride around the Lake yesterday on the steamer Stanford and had a glorious a time as was ever mortal man's lot to enjoy!"

Tahoe Tattler: July 21, 1881
"A trouting contest took place yesterday evening between two ladies and two gentlemen. The contest was vigorously fought for, as the losing party were to stand for supper. The ladies, being under the management of a popular fishing expert of Tahoe, came out victorious with a total catch of twenty while the other party only managed ten. The gentlemen return to their respective homes in Sacramento this evening disgusted with fishing tackle, likewise with themselves."

Tahoe Tattler: August 6, 1881
"Miss Anna Head is one of the most noted lady swimmers of this coast, and if this fine weather lasts, she may try her skill in the Lake, and thus refute the common idea that good swimmers are not able to navigate these waters. Lake Tahoe water is about six degrees warmer than the average temperature of the ocean and there is no reason why swimming should not become a very popular amusement here."

Tahoe Tattler: July 19, 1881
"Twelve hundred copies of the Tattler are distributed over the world every week, and the number is sure to enlarge. Citizens of the Lake...you who are doing business here...can you estimate the advantages to be derived from advertising in such a paper? Our business is now large but human nature is not easily satisfied, so send in your subscriptions and advertisements. Scatter the facts about our lake over the world, and you will soon have more travelers than our stages, steamers and hotels can attend to. Hurrah now everybody!"
Author's note; I guess it worked!

CHAPTER TWENTY-TWO

HEAVEN ON EARTH
A History of
Heavenly Valley Ski Area

Lake Tahoe has been a favorite destination for local Washo and Paiute Native Americans for hundreds of years. In one high valley, up among the tallest peaks of the region, they found abundant game and a cool stream fed by large snowfields. They would later describe this area to the first white settlers as "heavenly" and it would come to be known as the 'Heavenly' Valley.'

Heavenly Valley became the name given to South Lake Tahoe's first large ski development. Known as Heavenly Mountain today, the south shore of Lake Tahoe is blessed to have one of the premier ski areas in the country. With 30 chairlifts, 4,800 acres of skiable terrain, and 3,500' vertical drop, the legendary Lake Tahoe ski resort ranks among the best. Operating since 1955, Heavenly is a fixture on Lake Tahoe's south shore and has provided memorable experiences for millions of guests.

In the U.S., interest in skiing took off after World War Two. Winter sports were neither organized or regulated then, and people would use any (preferably accessible) steep slope with sufficient snow to make a few turns. With its location up against the base of the Carson Range, South Lake Tahoe's inclined slopes were readily recognized by would be skiers and winter enthusiasts. They came to South Lake Tahoe to test their skiing skills by day and enjoy South Lake Tahoe's gaming and entertainment action at night.

A few businessmen, that were already involved in the South Shore's hospitality trade, saw a good opportunity in developing an official ski area to draw more people to the Lake during the winter months. Straight down what we now know as Ski Run Boulevard, Messrs. George Cannon, Curly Musso, Chris Kuraisa, and Rudy Gersick cleared a few trees, had the slopes groomed, and put up a few rope tows. They called it Bijou Park Skiway. It proved popular from the start, and services were quickly expanded to include a warming hut, ski rental, a few ski instructors, floodlights for night skiing, and a straight, groomed run of about 1,000 feet long. The ski area even built a ski jump. The only real drawback was the ski run ended right at Highway 50, and as traffic on the road increased and skiers became faster and more daring, the "meeting" of the ski run and busy highway became downright dangerous.

Some suggested a ski bridge be built over Highway 50, but the operators decided to move the ski area to a safer location away from the well-traveled highway. The original Heavenly Valley opened in December of 1955 further east and north of Ski Run Blvd.

With improved winter snow removal on the state's highways and promotional tie ins with the Nevada casinos, visitation at Heavenly Valley continued to grow. In 1968, Heavenly opened its Nevada side, making it the first ski area to span two states.

Today, Heavenly Mountain Ski Area can safely and efficiently handle thousands of people a day. Average snowfall is about thirty feet per year, but just in case…Heavenly can boast it has the largest snow making capacity of any ski area in the United States. Heavenly…Lake Tahoe!

Early skiers used whatever steep slope they could find to test their downhill skills.

Heavenly Valley Ski Resort Set To Open Today

New Chair Lift Due Dedication Rite Near Bijou

BIJOU, Calif., Dec. 14. — The Heavenly Valley chair lift, described by one expert as "the best ski lift in the United States," will be formally unveiled to the winter sports public this weekend.

Dee Mowrer, field engineer for Heron Engineering Company of Denver, heaped the extravagant praise on the Heavenly Valley lift on completion of the customary safety tests.

Rides on the double chair lift will be offered free of charge Thursday, opening day. The entire Highway 50 area is geared for a good-sized "pre-

| Ski areas and gaming partnered in their promotion. | Operators promoted the ski area year round. | The original ski area at Ski Run Blvd. was relocated in 1955. |

CHAPTER TWENTY-THREE

Tales Along
LAKE TAHOE SHORES

AN UPHILL CLIMB
The Incline Tramway

Another little-known piece of Lake Tahoe history is also one of its most interesting. The Incline "Railway" was a narrow gauge, very short and very steep "railroad" on Lake Tahoe's northeast shore.

The great Comstock Lode had a voracious appetite for lumber. In the 1880s, Lake Tahoe had what seemed like an unlimited supply of trees. The cost of getting them to their destination at Virginia City was the key to a profitable operation. Log flumes were used to speed the lumber down off the mountains to the rail lines below, but getting the wood from the mills at Tahoe's lakeshore to the flumes required a lot of "horsepower."

In the early 1880s, Walter Hobart was one of two major lumber barons (the other was D.L. Bliss) that operated in the Lake Tahoe Basin. In 1878, Hobart formed the Sierra Nevada Wood and Lumber Company. The forest lands he cut from were mostly around the Lake's north end, which he purchased or leased for $2.50 to $12.50 per acre. The giant trees were hauled or rafted to Sand Harbor, where Hobart operated a steam powered sawmill that churned out 40,000 board feet of lumber a day. The finished lumber, railroad ties, and cut fuelwood from the mill had to get to the rail landing in the Washoe Valley, where it was loaded on to the V & T Railroad and hauled to Virginia City.

A wagon road was built up from the Washoe Valley, crossed the Carson Range at 8,000-feet, then zigzagged down the west slope to lake level. When an enthusiastic reporter observed, "the trip over this new road is second only to a visit to Yosemite," enthusiastic Lake Tahoe boosters retorted, "Yosemite? Why we buried the equal of that furrow a million years ago in the middle of our bottomless lake."

Hauling the wood up the road to the flume was extremely expensive and inefficient. Hobart hired John Overton to run his mill and oversee the transporting of the wood.

The flume that sped the wood down off the mountain was fed by water that was brought by box flume from Marlette Lake…high on the mountain and a few miles south. The water from Marlette Lake dumped into a 4,000-foot tunnel that was blasted straight through the granite of the Carson Range from the Tahoe side to the Washoe Valley side, where its water fed into the V-flume.

The tunnel was originally built as part of the water supply for Virginia City and Gold Hill that came from Marlette Lake (see chapter 17).

As part of the wood delivery system, Hobart and Overton built their pièce de resistance…the Great Incline of the Sierra Nevada. A double set of narrow-gauge tracks, eighteen feet in overall width, was engineered by Overton to run straight up the mountain from a landing next to the mill, to the west portal of the tunnel. Cross ties were spiked to a solid log bed upon which the rails were spiked. Lumber and cordwood cars rolled along the track.

The cars were cantered to keep the loads somewhat level as they were hauled up the steep incline. An 8,000 foot long, one and one eighth inch diameter cable fed around two massive twelve-foot diameter, eight spoked bull wheels. The wheel at the top was driven by a gigantic sprocket and gear turned with a 40-horsepower steam engine embedded into a granite walled powerhouse.

Twelve combination cordwood and lumber cars were used to haul the wood. Each car could haul one and one-half cords of wood or an equivalent amount of lumber. The tramway would pull two loaded cars up the steep ascent while the empties descended on the adjoining track, their weight assisting the overloaded steam engine.

The tram would climb a 1,400-foot incline over its 4,000-foot length. In places, the degree of gradient was 67%. It would take about 20 minutes for a full load to be pulled up the incline, allowing for about 300 cords (or their equivalent) per day. By the fall of 1881, Hobart's logging/tramway operation employed 250 laborers. By 1884, the settlement was classified with its own voting precinct and post office.

The ingenuity of the Hobart company was proudly on display with the Great Incline. It drew the attention of the traveling public's fancy, and the owners of Lake Tahoe steamships ran special excursions from several points on the Lake to Incline so that sightseers could see the modern marvel for themselves.

But as is often the case, just as the Great Incline came into its full capability, the silver on the Comstock began to decline, and the demand for wood lessened. Logging slowed down so much that by the fall of 1897, nothing was left of the engineering masterpiece but stripped forest lands, the deep scars of logging roads, and a maze of crumbling flumes.

When one is on Lake Tahoe's west shore looking east, huge vertical scars stripe the mountainside's west face above the Sand Harbor area. These scars have been caused over the past 140 years by the washing out and overflow of the Marlette Lake box flume, winding 1,800-feet above the Tahoe shore. In the 1890s, steamship captains would tell their patrons the scars were actually caused by fun loving black bears that would scoot down the steep hillside when coming out of their winter hibernation. This tall Tahoe tale still circulates, and the scars are often referred to as "Bear Slides."

Walter Hobart himself was a person of much interest. Born to a wealthy East Coast family, he attended Yale University. Hobart developed a reputation for "going the way of the flesh," with his penchant for alcoholic spirits, fine food, and sparkling women. There is a tale of him riding the cow catcher on the front of one of his logging locomotives, clutching a guitar in one hand and passing around a five pound box of chocolates in the other, while the engine swayed and puffed its way along the tracks to Sand Harbor.

Hobart owned a small fleet of ships upon which he plied across Lake Tahoe's waters. He had practically every electrical contrivance known to humanity at the time installed in his ships, keeping a small army of mechanics busy all summer. He loved to test his ships' swiftness against other fine boats of Tahoe's wealthy in yearly races. If you fell into his disfavor, he was known to name one of his outhouses after you.

![The upper bull wheel that pulled the loaded wood carts to the top of the tram is still visible today from a hike near Sand Harbor.]

The upper bull wheel that pulled the loaded wood carts to the top of the tram is still visible today from a hike near Sand Harbor.

Walter Hobart passed away in 1933. His family sold a good portion of his Lake Tahoe property to wealthy and eccentric George Whittell Jr. in 1936 (see chapter twelve). Whittell eventually acquired 45,000 acres of the Lake Tahoe Basin and nearly all the Nevada side shoreline. In 1959, Whittell sold 14 ½ square miles of the northeast corner of his property to developers. This eventually became the community of Incline Village, the second most populous town at Lake Tahoe.

The upper bull wheel at the top of the old Incline is still there and can be accessed by a moderate hike. Its worn and dilapidated state today contrasts sharply with its prideful past, when it worked day and night contributing significantly to the success and glory that was the Comstock Lode.

To learn more about the hike to the remnants of the Incline bull wheel: https://www.nevadalandtrust.org/news/bull-wheelincline-flume-trail

One of the few known photos of the Incline Railway-Tram, that hauled firewood and lumber from Lake Tahoe's shore 1,400' up the side of the mountain.

Tales Along
LAKE TAHOE SHORES

CHAPTER TWENTY-FOUR
WHEN YOUR SHIP COMES IN
Lake Tahoe's Early Maritime History

Lake Tahoe's maritime history is almost as extensive as the passages of yesteryear that have taken place on terra firma.

Washo people used dugouts and skiffs to travel about the Lake's expansive waters for hundreds of years. Though they likely traveled close to shore, evidence suggests that traveling from one end of the Lake to the other was not uncommon. Fishing was a very important food source for the Washo, and being on the water allowed them to maximize their piscary.

A road completely around Lake Tahoe did not materialize until 1913, and, even then, it was a long, rough, and bumpy trip. Gliding along over the shimmering sapphire expanse of Lake Tahoe in a boat or ship was infinitely smoother…except of course during a big and windy storm.

As early as 1856, there were mentions in various newspapers of ships being built for use on Lake Tahoe. But the first recorded appearance of a modern ship on the Lake was not until 1860. Teamster George Gordinier freighted two 28-foot whale boats over Johnson Pass (now Echo Summit) for two different Lake Tahoe businessmen. 1860 was a very busy time on the "Bonanza Road" as men and freight were streaming east to the newly discovered Comstock Lode of Virginia City and Gold Hill. It must have been quite a site to see these behemoths being transported over a steep and narrow wagon road, and quite an accomplishment by Gordinier to successfully do so.

Also in 1860, Homer Burton from Tahoe City placed a sizable sailing ship dubbed the *Edith Batty* on Lake Tahoe. The *Edith Batty* was the first ship at Tahoe to carry the mail…a very important task for the often-isolated Lake residents. The good ship would also carry much needed supplies into the Lake's remote reaches. She was a welcome sight among many with her sails spread grandly in a Tahoe zephyr, but because the breezes of the lake were a bit unpredictable, the *Edith Batty* operated on a fairly irregular schedule. She called on at least eight communities and would take as long as a week to make the entire circle route to various ports on the Lake. The *Edith Batty* served her Tahoe community well, but as faster ships began to arrive, her services were used less and less. She was relegated to fishing and leisure trips by 1870.

Over the next several years, other sailing ships appeared, but it was the use of steam power that soared to the forefront of Lake Tahoe cruising. The first steamship, the *Governor Blaisdel*, arrived at Lake Tahoe in 1864. The *Governor Blaisdel* was named after Nevada's first governor. The *Governor* carried passengers and cargo, and also tugged log rafts across the Lake for Tahoe's Glenbrook lumber mills. She served proudly in her varying capacities until

89

1877, when a wicked Lake Tahoe storm sent her crashing into the shore, breaking apart on Glenbrook Bay.

The 55-foot *Emerald* was the next steamer to ply Lake Tahoe's waters. She was hauled by train as far as Truckee on a flatbed rail car. The torturous 14 ½ mile trip up the Truckee River Canyon to Tahoe City was not as easy. Twenty-four oxen struggled mightily to move the behemoth to the Lake up the rough stage road. She was the envy of all mariners of the Lake when first launched. Many claimed she looked as sleek as a railroad parlor car with her twenty-eight feet of cabin and her square drop windows. And at 12-MPH under a full head of steam, she was twice as fast as any other Lake Tahoe ship at the time. The *Emerald* spent her final days as a tow ship for log rafts and met her final demise during a turbulent 1881 lake storm.

Additional steamships appeared at the Lake over the next few years. The Lake mail contract was rotated among several of these ships, often depending on which was the fastest vessel at the time.

Among the most noteworthy of these steamships was the *Meteor*. Commissioned by lumber baron D.L. Bliss, the *Meteor* was built specifically as a tow boat for Bliss' lumber company in 1876. The *Meteor* was the first "iron-hulled" ship introduced on the west coast. The 80' x 10' metal hull was constructed by a Delaware ship builder, dismantled with the pieces numbered, and then shipped by rail to Carson City and reassembled at the Lake. Many local observers didn't believe a ship so heavy would float. "Why…that slim iron slipper is going to sink like a rock if Bliss makes the mistake of launching the vessel instead of turning it into quarters for his millhands," said the editor for the *Nevada Appeal*. He was proven wrong.

The *Meteor* not only stayed afloat, her powerful 16-foot boiler propelled the log tug along the Lake at an unheard of 24-mph. She was the pride of the Bliss family with dignitaries of all sorts treated to excursion trips in between her log raft hauling. Because of her speed, she frequently carried the mail around to the Lake's ports as well.

The *Meteor* was often operated in the darkness of night and was said to have been an unforgettable sight. Accounts recalled; as the low hulled vessel glided along the water in darkness under a full head of steam, flaming sections of pine as big as a man's fist erupted from the *Meteor's* stack, giving her the appearance of a giant Roman candle as she churned away in the darkness.

The *Meteor* served reliably and dutifully for 52 years. She was retired to Tahoe City where she sat for 11 years. The Bliss family eventually had her towed out to a spot on the Lake that was in a direct line between Tahoe City and Glenbrook. Her sea cocks were opened and one of the longest serving ships on the Lake sank to a watery grave.

One of the most noteworthy of all of Lake Tahoe's many ships was the S.S. *Tallac* (she finished her career as the *Nevada*). She was originally brought to Lake Tahoe by Lucky Baldwin, to ferry his guests from Tahoe City to his luxury hotel on the Lake's south shore in 1890. She too was of a metal hull. The *Tallac* suffered a major fire just a year later. She was taken to Tahoe City, removed from the water and transported to a San Francisco boatworks. Not only was she rebuilt, but Baldwin had her length extend from 60' to 85'. When she reappeared at the Lake, Baldwin promoted her as the "handsomest steamer on the Pacific Coast."

The Lucky Baldwin "touch" was found throughout the ship. The cabin was finished with teak, cherry, ash, and black walnut, and her staterooms' plush seats were appointed in silk brocade. A large open cockpit on the afterdeck was covered by an awning and was a favorite location for her passengers to enjoy the Lake.

The *S.S. Tahoe*, or as it was also known, "the Queen of the Lake," was Tahoe's grandest steamship of the era. It was 168 feet long and contained a main travel compartment, parlor, and staterooms. It carried up to 200 passengers in addition to mail and freight. On a bright June day in 1896, a huge crowd gathered at Glenbrook to watch the big ship's maiden run. She was covered from bow to stern with bunting, flags, and assorted adornments. A brass cannon boomed as she slid down the launch rails. The *Emerald II*, *Meteor,* and *Tallac* were all present and sounded their whistles. Glenbrook's sawmills chimed in with their own raucous salute.

She was the epitome of luxury. There were many fond memories of guests dancing aboard the *Tahoe* under a moonlit night, with late night stops at McKinney's Resort and the Tallac House, where passengers disembarked at the over-water club houses.

As roads around Lake Tahoe were improved, and automobiles in general became more and more reliable, travel on Lake Tahoe by ship fell into decline. The *S.S. Tahoe* was one of the last commercial pleasure craft at the Lake, being scuttled off the Glenbrook shore in 1940.

Today, there are still a few vessels that provide a memorable and once in a lifetime experience on Lake Tahoe's enchanted waters. From catamarans, to paddle wheelers to classic wooden boats, there are several ways to get out on the water to choose from. For more information please visit: https://visitlaketahoe.com/?s=boat+tours

The *S.S. Emerald* was the second steamship to ply on Lake Tahoe's water.

The *S.S. Meteor* was the first iron hulled vessel in the entire Western United States. Many said she would sink as soon as she was launched. She served reliably and stayed afloat on Lake Tahoe's waters for 52 years.

The *S.S. Tahoe* was one of the largest and most luxurious ships to have glided over Lake Tahoe's waters.

Tales Along
LAKE TAHOE SHORES

CHAPTER TWENTY-FIVE
JEHU OF LAKE TAHOE
The Legend of Hank Monk

Hank Monk was one of the most famous stagecoach drivers of the American West, and his route operated right here in the Lake Tahoe region. Though his "driving" skills may not have been the safest, no one could argue that Hank's runs weren't among the fastest…and probably the most entertaining as well. And his ability to keep a straight face no matter the experience, added to the humor.

Henry James Monk was born in Waddington, New York around 1832. Even as a young man, it quickly became apparent that "Hank" had a natural ability when it came to handling horses. It is said as a preteen he displayed his prowess handling eight horses abreast during a town parade.

Some historians claim Hank landed his first job driving a stage at age 12. Other accounts have him being a few years older. Whatever the truth, Hank Monk was hired to be a stage driver at a very young age. He was given a regular route between Waddington and Massena, New York, a distance of 17 miles. Though not a difficult route, he displayed his stage driving skills aptly, and everyone said Hank was a "natural."

When President James Polk announced to the country in December of 1848 that gold had been discovered in California, Hank, along with a good number of the rest of his countrymen, was struck with gold fever and began to make plans to make his way west. His mother, Polly, put a kibosh on Hank leaving New York at such a young age, but by 1852, the quest for easy riches over came Hank, and he became westward bound.

It remains unclear if Hank spent much time actually prospecting for gold, but he fairly quickly impressed the folks at the California Stage Company. He landed steady employment driving a six-horse stagecoach from Sacramento to Auburn.

A few years later, Hank found work with the Overland Stage Company, and took over driving the Virginia City-Carson City route. At the same time, he also worked for the Pioneer Stage Company driving stagecoaches between Carson City and Glenbrook, which was the center of Lake Tahoe commerce at the time.

Hank Monk was very charming and personable. He could strike up a conservation with just about anyone and could weave a good story like a beautiful piece of tapestry. The Comstock Lode was at its peak during this time and drew many influential and well-known Americans to the area. Among Hank's many VIP guests were General William Tecumseh Sherman and President Rutherford B. Hayes. Hank built himself quite a reputation across the west for his stage driving prowess…and storytelling skills.

Many 19th century visitors to Lake Tahoe had heard so much of the legendary Monk, they specifically requested to ride with him. One of these aficionados was General and ex-President of the U.S., Ulysses S. Grant. On an around the world tour in 1877, he visited Lake Tahoe arriving by boat at Glenbrook. Grant requested to ride in a stagecoach driven by Hank Monk. Part way into the trip Grant asked Hank if he could take the reins of the team of horses. Allowing him to do so for a few minutes, Hank soon took back the reins from the ex-President telling him, "General, you may be a tolerable good fellow to run a government, but I'll be damned if you was cut out for a stage driver."

But it was a trip Hank spent with literary giant and *New York Tribune* newspaper editor Horace Greely, that brought him the most notoriety and publicity.

On July 30, 1859, Greely was in Genoa, Nevada running late for a speech that he was meant to give in Placerville later that day. As he boarded Hank's stage, he asked if it would be at all possible to get over the Sierra Nevada Mountains in time for his speaking engagement in Placerville. Hank assured Greely he would get him there with time to spare.

As the story goes, Hank set off with Greely at breakneck speed. The horses were pushed for all their worth along the Carson River up to Hope Valley, then swiftly over Luther Pass as Greeley bounced around in the coach and held on for his life. Hank drove the coach up steep Meyers Grade and on to Strawberry where he got fresh horses.

Strawberry was the last telegraph station on the way to Placerville, and Greely was still concerned if he would make it in time for his speech. He asked Hank again if he should wire ahead that they could be late. As the coach lurched forward in a cloud of dust…Hank called back to his VIP passenger, "I'll get you there!"

Hank roared down the South Fork of the American River canyon in his stage. Greely held on for dear life, peering frighteningly out the stage window at the steep drop offs as they rounded curve after curve at breakneck speeds.

Twelve miles before they reached Placerville, a welcoming committee met the stage and took Greely the remaining distance into town. Later that day, when the two met up again in town, the grateful (but still a little shaken) Greely offered to buy Hank a new suit.

Greely sent the story of his "fast trip" to Placerville with Monk to his newspaper back in New York. In it he recounted, "Yet at this breakneck rate we were driven for not less than four hours or 40-miles, changing horses every ten or fifteen and raising a cloud of dust through which it was difficult at times to see anything."

Greely's story was very well received and read and recirculated many times. Hank became even more famous from the Greely trip and was interviewed several times about it. In one of those interviews, he was quoted as saying, "I looked into the coach and there was Greeley, his bare head bobbing, sometimes on the back and then on the front of the seat, sometimes in the coach and then out, and then on the top and then on the bottom, holding on to whatever he could grab." Today, the story mainly lives on in

Mark Twain's tongue-in-cheek telling of the tale in his book, *"Roughing It."*

No matter his legendary skills as a master stagecoach driver, Hank was almost as well known, at least around his home in Carson City and the Carson Valley, for his ability to consume a great deal of adult beverage. There is one account that appeared in the book *Saga of Lake Tahoe:* "Monk drank so much hard spirits that he often forgot what he was doing, when it came to incidental tasks connected with staging, and fed whiskey to the horses and watered himself, thus becoming accidentally sober enough to handle the inebriated team."

Another story told about the day Hank was traveling to the top of Kingsbury Grade in a stage and was confronted by a robber. He was so surprised by the event, he threw the whiskey bottle that he was drinking from at the robber's head, knocking him out. Hank climbed down off his seat, gathered up his bottle of whiskey, put the robber in the stage, and delivered his new passenger to the sheriff at Friday's Station at Stateline, NV.

Hank Monk fell ill in the winter of 1883, and, after a brief battle, he passed away from pneumonia. The legendary stage driver and drinking man was given a fitting obituary in the *Territorial Enterprise* newspaper; "Hank Monk, the famous stagecoach driver is dead. He has been on the downgrade for some time. On Wednesday his foot lost its hold on the brake and his coach could not be stopped until, battered and broken on a sharp turn, it went into the canyon, black and deep, which we call death…"

Hank Monk was missed by all who knew him. He was known to be kind to everyone and spoke ill of no one…and he is a legend in the annals of Lake Tahoe and Western Nevada history.

Note: in the title of this chapter, "Jehu" is a biblical term referring to King of Israel, Jehu that "he drives furiously" (II Kings 9:20). In the 17th century, English speakers began using jehu as a generic term meaning "coachman" or, specifically, "a fast or reckless coachman." That moniker seemed perfectly to describe Lake Tahoe's legendary Hank Monk.

A stagecoach similar to what Hank Monk would have driven. Carson City, NV.

Hank Monk was one of the most legendary stagecoach drivers of the West.

Hank Monk gained such notoriety that Carson City composer J.P. Meader wrote a music score about the legendary stagecoach driver in 1878.

CHAPTER TWENTY-SIX

TRAPPED IN ICE
The Stranded Southern
Pacific Streamliner-1952

The winter of 1951-1952 was one of the most severe on record (see chapter twenty-one). Snow piled up so deep that residents at Lake Tahoe and Truckee had to use their second story windows to exit their cabins. The California and Nevada snow removal crews were working around the clock and still found it difficult to keep the mountain roads open.

On Sunday morning January 13, 1952, the pride of the Southern Pacific Railroad's (SP) passenger division…the *City of San Francisco* streamliner, was already 22 hours behind schedule when it pulled out of Norden Station just west of Donner Pass. Heavy, deep snows had slowed traffic along this mainline to a snail's pace as rotary plows struggled to keep the tracks open. Veteran Engineer Tom Sapunor and Fireman Gordon Painter made use of the forced stop at Norden to top off the water for the locomotive's steam generators…just in case.

There had already been trouble on SP's busy route across the Sierra Nevada Mountains. The day before, an SP's passenger train stalled in a huge snowslide ten miles west of Norden. The train had to be dragged out and sent back down east to Reno. The impact into the snow slide was so great the windows of the locomotive shattered sending a spray of glass into the engine's cab, injuring the engineer and crew.

The big diesel locomotives gained speed as Sapunor opened the throttle as it pulled out of Norden. The howling head winds were so strong that even on the downgrade, forward momentum was hindered. At Donner Summit, the weather station registered wind speeds at over 100 miles an hour.

Plowing through snow which rose to 12-feet on the upslope and 6-feet deep on the down, the streamliner, now barely crawling, made its way part way around a rocky point…and directly into a massive avalanche of snow that had just come down. The train's motors whined, and the diesel engines rose in crescendo.

"That's it!" shouted Sapunor. "We can't make it!" Reversing the train's motors, the engineer attempted to back his train out of the towering drift, but it would not move. The *City of San Francisco* was stalled, and immediately began freezing up underneath her entire length. Sapunor instructed one of his crew to walk to the nearest emergency phone at Yuba Pass to call for help. The crew member told SP dispatch of their situation.

The snowbound train wasn't the only dilemma facing the SP. Heavy rains in the Central Valley were causing flooding on some of the SP's lines. SP Superintendent M.L. Jennings immediately began dispatching trains and rotary snowplows from the east and west to assist the stalled train. Assistant Superintendent Bob Miller at Norden (the closest station) promised a rotary plow would be there in short order.

With the frigid temperatures, ferocious winds, and unrelenting snow, the *City* froze up fast. Brake rigging, under-floor tanks…everything became frozen solid. The storm raged on with no signs of easing up. Rotary plows approached the frozen train from both sides of Donner Summit. The first one got within fifty feet…and stalled. The desperate men used hand shovels to dig the rotary out. The freed rotary plow approached the *City* within a few feet and attempted to pull it free…but it would not budge.

The Southern Pacific streamliner became solidly entombed in ice within hours of becoming stalled.

A rotary plow made it up from the west. It too attempted to pull the train free of its icy tomb, but the ice held it in an unmovable grip. Mechanical breakdowns on some of the rotaries exacerbated the situation by blocking other equipment from approaching the train. The snowstorm was so severe, that the California Highway Department could not keep U.S. Hwy. 40, which paralleled the railroad tracks in many places, open.

The first night closed in on the *City* with its 236 passengers and crew. Lucky and efficacious that Engineer Sapunor had filled those diesel steam-heat generator boilers to capacity. The boilers were sorely needed to keep passengers and crewmen warm and alive.

At first, the mood of the passengers was downright jovial. They were confident they would be freed before too long and relished in the novelty of their situation. Some crewmen had lugged bags of coal to the train through massive snowdrifts to aid in keeping the passengers warm. Train crews dug and pulled and pushed…all to no avail in attempts to free the entombed train.

The morning of January 14 was bitterly cold. A rescue train had come up within eight miles from the west with food, doctors, and nurses, but the rails remained blocked with snow and ice. Rotaries were storming the mountain, not once or twice, but again and again. They often got stuck themselves and had to be dug out by the men with shovels. Another avalanche crashed down from the mountain, overturning one of the rotaries and killing engineer Raymond Holland. And the blizzard never let up. The temperature was down to 2 degrees, and with the gale force wind it was distressing and dangerous.

At first, a party atmosphere prevailed among the passengers. But as time went on and they remained stranded, a gloomier outlook prevailed. Note the lady on the left, feet wrapped in towels to stay warm.

Fortunately, there happened to be a doctor among the 236 passengers and crew. His services were required when one of SP's crew, who had worked through the night in the rescue attempts, crumpled from extreme fatigue.

Southern Pacific was trying everything humanly possible to affect a rescue. So were many others. The Sixth Army, under Major G.C. Cotton, loaded all terrain weasels on flatcars and took them to the closest point they could drive the trucks. But the weasels could not negotiate the deep snows. The Pacific Gas & Electric Company's Sno-Cat got through, but one double-trucked track-laying vehicle could not take 236 people out. But it was able to bring in supplies…as well as word of rescue efforts by rail, highway, and air. PG&E's Sno-Cat operator Jay Gold, later died of sheer exhaustion.

The U.S. Army sent all terrain "weasels" that unsuccessfully tried to access the ice bound train.

With everything frozen, SP's Assistant Road Foreman of Engines, Charlie Carroll, recognized an important but irksome task. He organized a latrine patrol, and with cans from the baggage car, he and the engineers, firemen, conductors, a brakeman, and a baggageman performed the necessary operation.

On the second night, the steam-heat generators gave out, and the SP crew rigged up an external generator. But soon, snow choked exhausts around the train's air-conditioning equipment under the cars caused obnoxious gases to enter the Pullmans. Passengers became feint and nauseous. The generator was turned off, and, fortunately, no passengers fell seriously ill.

January 16 broke calm and clear with only light winds. A Coast Guard helicopter soon appeared over the stranded train. Visions of food, supplies and perhaps a doctor descending by parachute with accurate news of a real rescue went through the mind of every passenger and crew. Supplies, medical aids, and food were dropped, but the doctor could not be safely parachuted…and still no rescue was in sight. Was it the calm before the next storm? A minor one broke at that moment.

"That cook! My third cook! He's crazy…look at him go!" This was the cry from the train's head chef. One of his helpers momentarily lost his nerve and dived out the window of the train into the massive snow drifts. Brave and

100

concerned passengers rescued the buried man. They brought him safely back to the train…and unbelievably, he returned to his duties in the kitchen.

Rotaries and rescue trains still could not reach the stranded train. Concern grew among SP officials about the possibility of another avalanche crashing down and pushing the *City* into the steep canyon below. Just such an event had occurred 42 years earlier in Washington State's Cascade Mountains. Ninety-six people were killed in that horrific train disaster that came to be known infamously as the "White Death."

THE SEATTLE STAR — HOME EDITION — THE SEATTLE STAR

SEATTLE, WASH., WEDNESDAY, MARCH 2, 1910.   ONE CENT

SURVIVOR SAYS SIXTY-FIVE WERE IN SLIDE

NONE CAN BE ALIVE NOW HE SAYS

HERE IS DEATH HILL, WHICH SENT TONS OF SNOW DOWN ON HEADS OF HELPLESS PASSENGERS

The terrible 1910 tragedy in Washington State, where 96 passenger and crew lost their lives while stranded in a snowbank, was fresh on the minds of Southern Pacific officials.

SP crew members had beaten down enough snow to create a crude footpath from the stalled train to a nearby and still closed U.S. Hwy. 40. But the California Highway Department had been working furiously, and on the morning of the third day of being stranded, an ecstatic voice came over the radio… "They're through! They got through! We can get out down the highway!" The Highway Department got 40 open." It was just a short walk of a few hundred yards through a perpendicular cut through solid ice and snow down to the highway.

Highway Department cars and private automobiles from Herschel Jones' Nyack Lodge crawled up the canyon, swung into the turnaround, and waited to affect the final rescue. Women and children made the jubilant exodus from the train protected from the stinging cold by pillowcases with eye holes cut in them. Blankets wrapped them against the weather as the passengers trudged across the icy path to safety.

The autos took the passengers, crews, and officials down the sheer-walled canyon to Nyack Lodge and on to the waiting rescue train at Yuba Gap. Steaks and all the trimmings were served to elated passengers. Doctors and nurses checked everyone over, but for the most part…all were OK.

Once the passengers were safe, SP brought in huge caterpillars and bulldozers from A. Teichert & Sons and Luntz Construction Company in Sacramento. After much effort and a lot of digging, the *City of San Francisco* was dragged free of Mother Nature's icy grip.

The rescue of the 236 passengers and crew aboard that train stranded in the Sierra Nevada Mountains that winter, was truly a heroic event of major proportions. Hundreds, if not thousands, of people worked tirelessly, some with little or no rest and risking their own lives, to ensure the safety of these marooned innocents. A very difficult situation…where a major tragedy was avoided.

The jubilant passengers were led down a beaten down snow path a few hundred yards to a cleared U.S. Hwy 40, where cars were waiting to take them to the safety of Nyack Lodge and the rescue train.

Once the passengers were rescued, heavy equipment and hundreds of men with shovels were brought in to free up the ice bound train.

CHAPTER TWENTY-SEVEN
DAM LAKE TAHOE
Big Plans for Tahoe's Water

To many, the damming of Yosemite's Hetch-Hetchy Valley is a manmade environmental disaster of the highest level. The serene valley (now a reservoir) has been compared of equal beauty to the epitome of nature's greatest temple, Yosemite Valley.

In the laser sharp focus of the loss of marvelous Hetch Hetchy, a significant story from California's long history of water conflict has almost been forgotten. Before the boosters of the growing metropolis of San Francisco ever set their sights on Hetch-Hetchy, Lake Tahoe was at the forefront of consideration for the City's (and much of Northern California's) water supply.

"Fanny Bridge" is one of the more popular manmade attractions at Lake Tahoe. Spanning the outlet of "Big Blue," at Tahoe City, legend says the bridge was named this for the all the "fannies" that can be seen from the road as gawkers stare over the edge into the crystal-clear sapphire waters of Lake Tahoe. But this spot has a deep and involved history far beyond the legend of the view of spectators' posteriors.

Like many historical California figures, Alexis Von Schmidt emigrated to California upon the announcement of the California Gold Rush in 1849. Von Schmidt was trained as a civil engineer and surveyor, and his ties to the Lake Tahoe area are extensive. Like most of those hoping to strike it rich, Von Schmidt didn't have much luck with prospecting for gold, and he returned to working as a surveyor.

Von Schmidt ended up in the San Francisco Bay area and helped engineer the city's first water system. He also helped design its famed cable car complex. He received extensive praise for his successful removal of Blossom Rock, an immense natural hazard to ships navigating San Francisco Bay. Von Schmidt also engineered and oversaw the construction of San Francisco's first dry dock. His contribution to San Francisco's development was unrivaled at the time.

Von Schmidt understood the importance for the city to have a reliable source for an adequate domestic water system, and that any future growth would be dependent upon finding one. He had become familiar with Lake Tahoe and thought it might well be the solution for meeting San Francisco's future water needs. He established the Lake Tahoe and San Francisco Water Works Company in 1865. Its stated purpose was to bring the water of Lake Tahoe to the Bay Area, a distance of 163 miles. He bought land at and around Lake Tahoe's outlet (the Truckee River) and constructed a small rock filled timber crib dam down just slightly below the outlet. Von Schmidt's dam would provide a steady supply of water for the downstream log flumes and lumber mills, while working on his grander project.

The dam caused problems from the start. The rising lake level flooded lakefront property owned by wealthy and politically powerful property owners. In 1890, the dam had been sold, and was rebuilt and enlarged by the Truckee River General Electric Company to provide a steady supply of hydroelectric power to the area.

But Von Schmidt was still focused on building his aqueduct. His plans called for constructing a larger dam at Tahoe's outlet, which would raise lake level by as much as 25-feet. Von Schmidt would also build a diversion dam about four miles downstream, where a six-mile canal would speed the water from the Truckee River to Squaw Valley (now Palisades Tahoe). Once there, the water would be carried through the granite mass of the Sierra Nevada through a five-mile tunnel to a tributary of the North Fork of the American River.

Once Lake Tahoe's waters were on the Sierra Nevada's west slope, a huge ditch (500,000,000 gallons a day capacity) would transport some of the water to the hydraulic mines at Forest Hill, Yankee Jim's, and other gold mining camps.

The bulk of the water would flow for twelve miles in the American River bed, and then diverted into a forty-mile stone lined canal that flowed to a huge reservoir to be constructed near Auburn. Sundry pipes and canals would provide water for Sacramento and Central Valley farms, and the main aqueduct would continue to San Francisco.

Von Schmidt proposed to San Francisco government officials that the City pay the majority of the costs with a ten-million dollar bond issue, and he would retain ownership of the water system. Many supported Von Schmidt and his ambitious project, and many more were adamantly opposed. Powerful Leland Stanford of the Central Pacific Railroad reached out to partner with Von Schmidt on his project. Stanford thought the monumental tunnel through the Sierra Nevada could be a joint water and railroad tunnel. Such a tunnel would greatly improve the rail line across the Sierra Nevada by easing the gradient, and eliminating the need for miles of costly snowsheds. In August of 1871, Von Schmidt announced the joint water/railroad tunnel had been surveyed and two gangs of workmen would soon begin boring from both ends of the tunnel. He hoped to have 400 workers on the project by the following spring, and was eager to begin using the ingenious compressed-air tunnel boring machine he had recently invented.

Von Schmidt's plans for damming Lake Tahoe continued to be met with earnest resistance. Many in San Francisco were opposed to footing the bill for a project that would be privately owned when completed. San Francisco's mayor and city attorney were also wary of possible lawsuits over water rights. And...the entire State of Nevada rose up in opposition to having water that ultimately flowed into their state (Pyramid Lake) be reversed and flow to the "greedy interests" of California.

Several legislative and legal efforts to stop any diversion of Lake Tahoe and the Truckee River were initiated by the Silver State. In 1900, Nevada Senator William Stewart proposed a Lake Tahoe National Park, hoping this designation would forestall any water diversions. Newspapers in Reno intimated that Von Schmidt might be well advised to hire armed men to protect his project. Hints at violence appeared more frequently in the editorial pages.

Von Schmidt continued with his efforts to develop a Lake Tahoe Aqueduct. His attempts surged and waned depending upon the current drought situation in California. He was nothing if not persistent, and he tirelessly lobbied to garner capital for his ambitious project from public or private sources.

Around that same time, the congressman from Nevada, Francis Newlands, began advocating for more irrigation in the western United States to further the settlement of farmers and ranchers in remote rural areas. His efforts were soon developed into what he called the "Truckee Irrigation Project." With President Theodore Roosevelt's full backing, the U.S. Reclamation Service (now Bureau of Reclamation) was formed. Its purpose was to develop water projects that would lead to homesteading and promote economic development. It's very first project…became known as the Newlands Project in honor of the congressman.

The project set out to gain rights and ownership of the existing, small, Truckee River General Electric Dam at Tahoe City. The top six feet of Lake Tahoe would be "regulated" by the Bureau, to maintain a constant supply of water to irrigate parts of western Nevada with the Truckee River.

The project moved forward, and soon the desert lands near Fallon, Nevada were being irrigated by Lake Tahoe water. Churchill County became the agricultural leader of Nevada. And…Pyramid Lake, the ending spot for the Truckee River (and part of the Paiute Native American Reservation), dropped by 87 vertical feet in the next 63 years.

Von Schmidt passed away in May of 1906. A month earlier, the old man watched from his Alameda home as San Francisco was ravaged by the three-day inferno touched off by the catastrophic San Francisco Earthquake. He must have thought the city had paid for its shortsightedness; Tahoe water might have saved it. But even after his death, his dream of the "grandest aqueduct" was kept alive.

James Waymire, a prominent San Francisco attorney, conducted a thorough study of the legal matters of building an aqueduct from Lake Tahoe to the Bay Area and concluded it stood on safe ground. He was also able to secure solid financial support for a Tahoe-Bay Area aqueduct. Waymire's plan focused on the financial benefits that would be derived by the massive amount of hydroelectric power such an aqueduct could produce. His plan called for a $42-million dollar investment. Waymire pointed out that California was a garden land compared to Nevada's limited agricultural prospects and therefore more "deserving" of the Truckee River-Tahoe water. Unexpectedly, before much progress was made, Waymire passed away on a trip east, where it was reported he was attempting to secure additional financing for his aqueduct.

With Waymire's death, the idea of obtaining Lake Tahoe water for San Francisco also met a mortal defeat. The City turned its attention to Lake Eleanor and the Hetch Hetchy Valley in Yosemite. Ironically, this project proved much more controversial. John Muir passionately fought attempts to dam Hetch-Hetchy for thirteen years, and according to some, its damming brought Muir's life to an end.

**San Francisco, 1870. The City by the Bay was already nearing its limit
on the amount of water available for its growing population.**

In 1908, the Stone and Webster Company…an eastern power syndicate, decided to expand its operations to the West Coast. It secured an option to purchase the Truckee River power company and its dam at Tahoe City. Stone and Webster began negotiations with the Reclamation Service to work out a deal where the power company would provide 200,000-acre feet of Tahoe water to supplement the Service's Newlands project which was already running short of water during the dry year of 1907. Incredibly, part of Stone and Webster's plan was to drill a tunnel from the Washoe Valley through the Carson Range to drain Lake Tahoe's water several hundred feet below its surface. Generators would be placed on the Washoe Valley side of the tunnel producing enormous amounts of electricity. The outflow from the subsurface "Tahoe Tunnel" would then flow into Washoe Lake for irrigation storage. Such a plan would have effectively stopped any outflow of Lake Tahoe water at Tahoe City. The Truckee River…would have been completely dried up.

The administration of President Taft nearly finalized a contract that would have allowed the outrageous plan to take place. A forester from the Department of Agriculture learned of the preposterous project and mustered an extensive opposition effort that lasted all the way until 1935. By then, Lake Tahoe's value as a destination for outdoor adventure and personal rejuvenation was firmly implanted in the American psyche, and no longer considered merely a resource to develop for industry and financial gain.

Von Schmidt's ambitious plans to change nature and move water highlighted the need for new government agencies that specialized in large public projects. How could political men (and eventually women) with little or no engineering knowledge evaluate the practicality and ramifications of such huge engineering projects? As a consequence, many new specialized agencies were created including water commissions, utility commissions, and environmental agencies to protect our precious natural resources. Today, the outflow of Lake Tahoe's Truckee River is still highly regulated.

Many groups (especially Native Americans) have been greatly and often grievously affected by efforts to control its natural flow. But when we reflect back on all the fanciful ideas of what "may have been" for Lake Tahoe and its valuable water…we can give thanks to have the Lake in as admirable state as we enjoy it today.

In addition to his Lake Tahoe/Bay Area water project, Alexis Von Schmidt (R) was also commissioned to survey the CA/NV state boundary in 1872. This iron monument was placed near Brockway on Tahoe's north shore.

Fanny Bridge at the Lake Tahoe/Truckee River outlet- Tahoe City.

The first dam built at Lake Tahoe's outlet was in 1870 to support the logging and lumber mill operations located downstream near Truckee.

The original dam at Lake Tahoe was replaced in 1890, and has seen many "improvements" since then.

Tales Along
LAKE TAHOE SHORES

CHAPTER TWENTY-EIGHT

OH THE PLACES WE GO!

Memories of Lake Tahoe Resorts

"Twenty years from now you will be more disappointed by the things you didn't do than by the ones you did do. So, throw off the bowlines, sail away from the safe harbor. Catch the trade winds in your sails. Explore. Dream. Discover." – Mark Twain

The magic elixir of Lake Tahoe's comforting and rejuvenating properties has been a powerful attraction since the first humans have laid eyes upon this shimmering blue sapphire. The deep forests, crystal clear waters, and majestic mountains brings us a sense of fulfillment and contentment during a visit to this mountain gem, and causes us all to seek its comforting nature often.

But, manmade elements can also have a special place in our hearts and minds...reminders of times well spent. Lake Tahoe has had many fine hostelries that have nurtured the weary urban visitor with warmth, comfort, and hospitality, and helped create special memories we treasure for the rest of our lives. Here is just a short list of some of those special places from Lake Tahoe's sentimental and nostalgic past.

Tahoe Tavern

D.L. Bliss saw an opportunity in tourism when his Lake Tahoe lumber business slid into decline in the 1890s. Loggers had cut almost 80% of the Tahoe Basin's trees in support of the Comstock Lode, but Bliss had wisely spared a bit of the original forest around Tahoe's outlet at Tahoe City.

Bliss laid rails from Tahoe City to Truckee, brought over his logging locomotives from Glenbrook, and purchased a few passenger cars. Lake Tahoe visitors would be able to take a train all the way to Tahoe's shore. At the same time, he began work on a hotel that would rival any in the country.

When the magnificent Tahoe Tavern opened for business in 1902, the diversity and durability of its success could not have been guessed at by its founder. The hotel featured running water, steam heat, electric lights, and excellent cuisine including perfectly prepared Tahoe Lake Trout. For those needing to conduct business while at the hotel, a telegraph line (and later a phone line) had been strung to the property. People flocked to the new luxury resort, and, for the next 62 years, visitors to Tahoe Tavern enjoyed the finest hospitality, comfortable accommodations, and created many cherished and lifelong Tahoe memories. To this day, the Tahoe Tavern's longevity stands as a record which no other Tahoe Basin caravansary has been able to surpass (though Harvey's Resort-Casino is coming close).

Tahoe Tavern near Tahoe City, boasted steamed heat, electric lights, running water, and was said to be the finest hotel between Denver and San Francisco.

Brockway Resort

At the north end of Lake Tahoe, right at the edge of the water line, sits a delightful spring of mineralized warmth. Washo people camped and enjoyed these hot springs for hundreds of years. In 1869, Billy Campbell and Henry Burke purchased 63 acres surrounding the hot springs. Seeing the popularity the springs had with area locals, they built a 40' x 60' hotel, five two-room lakeshore cottages, and a 20 square foot bathhouse over the hot springs that boiled out underneath a large rock. They christened their new resort, "Warm Springs Hotel."

The resort went through a number of different owners and names over the next many years. In 1900, Frank "Brockway" Alverson and his wife Nellie purchased the property and renamed the resort "Brockway Hot Springs." The new marketing slogan became "Top of the Map, Top of the List."

Despite their promotion and marketing, the Alversons struggled financially with the hot springs resort, and were forced into bankruptcy in 1909. They sold the resort to Melville Lawrence and Harry Comstock of Tallac for $9,000. Comstock managed Brockway through some of its most successful years, building a small casino and adding a nice dining room in 1917. That same year, he began making plans for a hot springs swimming pool.

Visitors to Lake Tahoe were enamored with the experience of soaking in the relaxing warm waters while enjoying a million-dollar view of the Lake, right at lake's edge. Brockway developed a fairly loyal following with many guests returning for a visit year after year. Comstock turned Brockway into one of the most sought-after destinations at Lake Tahoe.

After a 39-year run, Comstock passed away in 1954. His daughter Gladys and her husband took over managing the historic property. A fire destroyed the hotel in 1961, and Gladys closed the entire resort five years later. Brockway is now part of a private development, and the hot springs are closed to the public.

110

Brockway Hot Springs Resort offered hot pools right at Lake Tahoe water's edge. It was located on the north shore of Tahoe just west of the CA/NV state line.

Emerald Bay Resort

In the early 1880s, Dr. and Mrs. Kirby from Carson City took a cruise on a steamer to Emerald Bay while vacationing at Glenbrook. The Kirby's couldn't help but notice the presence of several other pleasure craft offering hundreds of sightseers a close up look of the glacier carved Lake Tahoe treasure. They saw a possibility, and the Kirby's purchased 500 acres of land fronting the northwest side of Emerald Bay, including Ben Holladay's property (see chapter six).

By 1884, the Kirbys had built a small hotel, a handful of rustic cottages, and a landing for steamers to dock. Guests to the Kirby's property could enjoy a pleasure party on their sloop, the *Mollie Brown,* or a special trip on their fast-racing yacht, the *Fleeter.* Mrs. Kirby raised a vegetable garden to provide fresh produce, and one single cow was barged over from Glenbrook to provide guests with fresh milk and butter.

Caretaker "Jack Tar" Sweetser kept a black bear as a pet at the property. The bear was popular with resort guests as well as steamers that would pull near to shore for their guests to observe the bear and his antics.

Dr. Kirby passed away in 1889. Mrs. Kirby remarried and, along with her new husband, kept the resort operating until they sold it to Nelson Salter, who had been in the hospitality business, having operated a store in Yosemite National Park.

In 1913, Tahoe's "Rim of the Lake" road circling Emerald Bay was completed. This was one of the most difficult sections of road constructed by the state, cutting across the near vertical slope of Maggie's Peak. In addition to being subject to recurring avalanches, the roadbed had to be blasted through solid granite. It is said it took 50 cases of dynamite to break apart one of the larger granite boulders. The road building became a popular sightseeing opportunity from boat excursions, as guests lined the rails to watch as thousands of tons of rock were blown into the air.

Salter made several improvements to the Emerald Bay Camp/Hotel, building more lodging and acquiring additional property. He brought in enhancements such as long-distance phone service, telegraph, daily mail, and express service. There were also rowboats for visitors and electrical lighting. As with many historic Lake Tahoe properties, Emerald Bay Camp/Hotel had thousands of guests that would return year after year. Many felt almost a proprietary interest in the property, thinking of it as their "own."

In 1947, Salter sold the resort to Joseph Watson, who operated it only six years until he sold it to the State of California who wanted the property to include in an Emerald Bay State Park. Watson leased some of it back and continued to operate it for a few more years. In 1957, the State of California removed the furniture and auctioned it off in Sacramento. The resort was officially marked closed in 1959, and all buildings were removed.

Emerald Bay Camp & Hotel helped guests create wonderful, lifetime memories of times well spent in the mountains at Lake Tahoe.

Hunter's Retreat/McKinney's Resort and Chambers Lodge

John McKinney had tramped the western shores of Lake Tahoe for years, looking for the perfect location for a hunting and fishing cabin. He finally settled on the south side of Upson Bay, protected by the prominence of Sugar Pine Point. In the summer of 1863, he opened Hunter's Retreat, comprised of a log cabin, tents, a pier, and four small fishing boats. The retreat catered to the wealthy of Virginia City, and grew to become quite popular.

John added more cabins and touted his location as the finest hunting and fishing in the Sierra Nevada. The guest services-oriented McKinney offered fishing boats free of charge to guests of his lodge, and it continued to grow in popularity. A newspaper scribe wrote, "It is situated in a pine grove and immediately on the shore of Lake Tahoe. Its genial host McKinney has accommodations for 60 guests and treats all his guests well."

McKinney came from a class of notable Lake Tahoe yarn spinners. One of his accounts he attributed to a Clem Anderson. "Clem," McKinney assured his visitors, "is a sober trustworthy sort of individual, and sure enough, he has seen a mammoth trout in the Lake I was told. It would go eight to nine feet in length with a girth the size of a pony barrel, and weigh in at about one hundred pounds when caught." Tall tales such as these provided McKinney with publicity and advertising he could not buy. If anyone questioned one of McKinney's stories, he would draw up his six-foot six frame and ask, "just show me where it warn't possible."

In 1889, McKinney's was one of the principal resorts on Lake Tahoe. His property now featured a dockside post office, an adjoining barber shop, and an over the water saloon. He would brag a man could "read his mail, get a shave and down several shots of whiskey while reclining in his waterside chair."

Unfortunately, as good as he was with his guests, he was a terrible businessman. He often carried past due accounts for years and/or wrote them off all-together. In 1892, he ended up deeply in debt and lost the property on a liquor bill foreclosure.

The new owners kept up the tradition of free fishing boats and tackle. They promoted the property to lowland visitors as, "No rattlesnakes, poison oak or harmful insects." In 1897, across the Lake at Glenbrook, D.L. Bliss offered the historic Glenbrook House free to anyone who would bear the cost of its removal. The McKinney's owners arranged to have the two and one-half story wayside inn, which had provided travelers along the great Bonanza Road a comfortable place to stay since the early 1860s, partially dismantled, loaded onto a cordwood barge, and transported across Lake Tahoe to their property, where it was set on a new foundation.

On the west shore, McKinney's Resort, later known as Chamber's Lodge, offered free fishing boats and tackle to use while on a visit to the historic property.

1920 saw the arrival of new owner Dave Chambers. Dave had been the manager of the Brockway Hot Springs Resort, and now would have his own resort property. He renamed it Chambers Lodge and kept up the tradition of exceptional guest services. He referred to his resort as, "an old-fashioned mountain-inn, but not a dressy place."

Dave Chambers became a familiar face on Tahoe's west shore. He had a reputation for being extremely kind and was always generous with his friends. He acted as the area's fire chief and took his position seriously.

Dave passed away in 1952. Over the next few decades, the resort changed ownership a number of times. Today, there is not much left of the original property. A blue-ribbon restaurant and bar known as Chamber's Landing provides a breathtaking view of the Lake in a casual and splendid atmosphere. And on a bluebird Tahoe day, gazing whimsically out at the magical and alluring Lake...one can still feel the marked presence of wonderful memories...and a time well spent...at Lake Tahoe.

Scene from Dining room. Bay View Resort. Emerald Bay.

Another fine old historic Lake Tahoe hostelry was the Bay View Resort, located at Inspiration Point above the south shore of Emerald Bay. It offered what was probably the finest views of any hotel or resort at Lake Tahoe. The area the resort stood at is now a U.S. Forest Service viewpoint along CA Hwy. 89.

CHAPTER TWENTY-NINE

THOSE THAT SURVIVED

The Heroes of the 1846 Donner Party

The tragic story of the Donner Party has been an important tale of American history for over 170 years. The horrific ordeal, where men and women resorted to unspeakable acts to survive, has been told and retold by historians and educators across the United States and even the world. This one aspect of the Donner Party's calamity has often become the primary focus when discussion of these forlorn pioneers takes place.

But there is far more to the tale of the Donner Party than the subject most often supposed. Forty-five of the eighty-nine people who headed onto the shortcut to California that winter of 1846-47 survived. Many historians have concluded that only a very small number of the desperate argonauts became an anthropophagite. Here is the "rest of the story," of their bravery, courage, and sheer will to survive.

The original Donner Party was made up of three families from Springfield, Illinois: George and Tamsen Donner and their five children, Jacob and Elizabeth Donner and their seven children, and George and Margret Reed and their four children. Accompanying the families were several hired teamsters as well as the Reed's domestic help, Eliza. With high hopes and little fear, the party left Springfield on April 15, 1846, with the dream of a better life in California.

The party joined a wagon train in Independence, Missouri, and their number swelled to almost three hundred people. Travel across the Great Plains was uneventful. When the wagon train came to an outpost known as Fort Bridger in what is now southwest Wyoming, the Donners, Reeds and a few dozen others were persuaded to leave the established Oregon Trail and take a new "shortcut" that was being promoted by a one Lansford Hastings. George Donner was elected the leader of this smaller group.

Hastings had not even traveled his purported shorter route, and the journey proved agonizingly difficult and slow. What was supposed to take a week to travel had taken a month. Several of the livestock used to pull the wagons ran off and could not be found. Wagons had to be abandoned, food supplies ran very short, and there was no water for a three-day stretch. Tempers flared.

Near the Humboldt River, James Reed became engaged in a severe argument with one of the teamsters, who then struck Reed and his wife Margret. In defense of his wife, Reed instinctively stabbed the man, who died there in the desert. For retribution for what had happened, Reed was banished from the party, and forced to leave his wife and four children. At first Reed refused to go, but Margret convinced him he should attempt to go ahead to Sutter's

Fort, over 500 miles away, to obtain food and supplies to bring back to his children who could be starving in the weeks ahead.

James and Margret Reed. James was banished from the Donner Party in the remote Nevada wilderness. Margret journeyed on with her four children alone. Reed made his way to Sutter's Fort where he organized a rescue party, and helped save the lives of many.

Reed took off across the Nevada desert as fast as his horse would travel. He quickly ran low of food, pushed his horse so hard it became lame, and he himself neared complete exhaustion. He traveled over 500 miles in 23 days and arrived at Sutter's Fort on October 28, 1846. He bought supplies and asked Sutter for men to help him with a rescue. But with the Mexican-American War being fought, there were no men available to help. Without help, Reed attempted to recross the Sierra Nevada Mountains the first week of November with food and supplies, but severe early winter snows blocked the route, and he was unable to proceed back to help his family.

Thanks to the help of Reed's hired teamsters, Margret, though devastated, was able to continue with the rest of the party. As they proceeded west across the Humboldt Sink, Margret and the others saw fresh snow on the high peaks ahead. The party made it to the Truckee Meadows (now Reno) and proceeded into the Truckee River Canyon. Light snow fell on the party even though it was only the end of October. They stopped to briefly rest at the edge of Truckee Lake (now known as Donner Lake and heretofore referred to as "Lake Camp"). The party noted there were crude cabins that had been built by those that passed this way a few years before.

Desperation began to take over many, as they ascended the steep slopes toward the pass, struggling through the deepening snows. Charles Stanton went ahead to scout the route. When he returned, he told the others they were within three miles of the pass, and, if they kept going, they would make it over that day. But complete exhaustion had overcome nearly everyone, and the party said they must rest and attempt the crossing the next day.

That night, the snow began to fall again…and it did not stop. Margret stayed up all night. She had covered the children with her shawl and had to shake off the fresh snow often. She fixed her gaze into the darkness as the snowflakes continued to fall. The next morning, over a foot of snow had fallen with drifts even higher. The party struggled through the deep powder and moved only a few hundred feet. After hours of strife, it was decided they had no choice but to return to the shelter of the crude Lake Camp cabins.

George and Jacob Donner were not with the main body of the party at that time. A few days earlier, George severely cut himself while trying to repair a broken axle on his wagon, and the two brothers stayed together, about six miles east of Lake Camp for George to recover. When the deepening snows began to fall, the Donners were stranded at what is now called Alder Creek, with no shelter save what they could make themselves.

Storms continued to bring more snow. A few in the main party made desperate attempts to cross over the mountains, all to no avail. On December 16, ten men and five women, the strongest of the group, left Lake Camp on handmade snowshoes in an attempt to get over the mountains to Sutter's Fort. The group took six days of very light food rations with them. Two days after they left, a "storm king" descended upon them. Gale force winds, bitter cold, and more snow pummeled the group. They huddled in the shelter of a snow hovel as best they could, but in their weakened state, some quickly perished. The storm raged for days, and the group was unable to move. More members in the party died, but those still alive eventually continued to make their way west as best they could. The party became known as the "Forlorn Hope."

The members of the party that remained at Lake Camp included Margret Reed and her four children. Margret prayed every day she would see her husband James return with food for their children. Food supplies became very low. A dismal Christmas Day came to Margret and her family. Just for this day, she had saved a few dried apples, some beans, a bit of tripe, and a small piece of bacon. When she gave it to her children, she told them to "eat as much as you wish on this special day."

Patrick and Elizabeth Breen and their seven children also remained at Lake Camp. Patrick began to keep a daily account of their time at the frozen and snowbound camp. His diary has become one of the best accounts of the Donner tragedy. On Christmas Day 1846, Breen wrote; "Offered our prayers to God this Christmas morning. The future looks bleak. The prospect is appalling but (we) hope in God, Amen."

At Sutter's Fort, James Reed was advised by Sutter that he should offer to assist Major John C. Fremont, who was leading American troops and militia in the Mexican-American War. Sutter told Reed he did not expect the War to last long, and perhaps Fremont would have some of his men help Reed once the fighting stopped, especially if Reed had curried favor with Fremont by volunteering to fight. Reed joined Fremont's militia and fought in a few battles in the San Jose area, January 1847.

By the middle of January, only seven (two men and all five women) of the fifteen original members of the Forlorn Hope group were still alive. The surviving members were severely weakened but fortunately came across a band of Native Americans (the Nisesan Tribe) who provided them with food and shelter. Only William Eddy had enough strength to continue. Leaving the remaining six with the Nisesan (and out of the snow), Eddy pressed on guided by two of the Native Americans.

10 men and 5 women attempted to reach Sutter's Fort in December 1846. It took them over a month to travel less than 100 miles. Only two men and all the women survived. They became known as the Forlorn Hope.

On Jan. 17, 1847, Eddy and the two Nieseans knocked on the door of a small cabin at Johnson's Ranch (near today's Wheatland). Seventeen-year old Harriet Ritchie opened the door and burst into tears at the sight of him. Eddy was emaciated, exhausted, and barely alive. The trail of his bloody footprints enabled rescuers from the Ranch to find and rescue Eddy's six companions on the trail behind him. It took thirty-three days and eight deaths before the Forlorn Hope was able to reach safety. Their tenacity set the rescue of the Donner Party in motion.

When news of the Forlorn Hope and the remaining stranded members still at Lake Camp reached Sutter's Fort, work on assembling a relief party greatly accelerated. Word of the desperate situation spread further to James Reed, who was in Yerba Buena (now San Francisco) at the time, trying to raise funds and volunteers for a rescue.

On February 5, 1847, the First Relief departed Sutter's Fort. The group was made up of twelve men and led by Captain Reason Tucker. Unbelievably, one of the twelve was William Eddy, who had barely made it to Johnson's Ranch as part of the Forlorn Hope just 18 days before. Eddy's wife and two children were still at Lake Camp, and he bravely attempted to return for their rescue.

The going was slow and dangerous. By the fifth day, the rescue party reached the first snow. It quickly became so deep that Captain Tucker concluded the pack animals could not continue, and the men would have to carry the food on their backs. Eddy, still extremely weak and unable to continue, led the pack animals back to Sutter's Fort.

In some places, the snow drifts were thirty-feet deep, and it became necessary to leave some of the supplies along the way as their packs were very heavy, and travel through the deep snow was extremely difficult.

On February 19th, after two weeks of travel, the First Relief finally arrived at Lake Camp. They were greeted by the destitute with a great deal of emotions. Children cried, grown men sat down and wept. The scene at the camp was gruesome. The bodies of those that had perished lay about on the snow. The living had not the strength to bury them.

Captain Tucker and the First Relief fed and nurtured the impoverished survivors. After three days, Tucker led those that felt strong enough through the snow across the mountains back towards Sutter's Fort. Twenty-three members of the Donner Party left with Captain Tucker. Margret Reed and all four of her children were among them. Storms stayed away, but tragically, two other children in the party perished.

After just two days, Margret's youngest children, Patty and Tommy, could not keep going. Margret said she would take her entire family back to Lake Camp, but Captain Tucker would not allow anyone who was capable of moving forward, to turn back. He instructed a member of the relief party, Mr. Glover, to take the children back to Lake Camp to stay with the others. Margret was beside herself with grief, guilt, and worry...but she kept on.

When James Reed had heard of the terrible condition the Donner Party was in, he immediately went to work assembling a second relief party. Reed was joined by two other Donner Party members (McCutchen and Miller), who had left the party before it entered the Sierra Nevada in an attempt to obtain supplies. The three men were all dedicated to saving as many of the people in their party they could. Ten other men (mostly soldiers who had fought alongside Reed a month before) joined Reed's Second Relief.

The Second Relief left Sutter's Fort on February 21, 1847. They met the first relief party headed west as they traveled. Reed, though greatly relieved to find his wife and two of his children, was grief stricken upon learning two of his children were still at Lake Camp. He and the second relief party double timed it the remaining distance. When he arrived at Lake Camp, he was overcome with joy when he saw Patty and Tommy were still alive.

Reed led seventeen of the Donner Party (including his two children) out of Lake Camp. Just a few days out they were caught in a vicious March storm, which caused Reed to go temporarily snow-blind. A third relief party followed a few days behind, led by a strengthened William Eddy. Another of the rescuers in this party, John Stark, a giant of a man, carried several children two at a time through the deep snow to safety. A fourth relief party did not arrive until April, finding only one remaining survivor.

Forty-seven of the eighty-nine that left to take the shortcut at Fort Bridger made it to Sutter's Fort. Interestingly, 75% of the women made it...less than 40% of the men survived. The entire Reed family (6) as well as all of the Breens (9) including daughter Isabella who was only one year old, made it through alive. All of the adults and most of the children in George and Jacob Donner's families, did not make it.

The tragic tale of the Donner Party was widely told and retold in newspapers, magazines, and by word of mouth. Emigration to California fell off sharply in 1847 and 1848, only to rebound in astronomical numbers in 1849, after it was announced gold had been discovered in the California foothills.

Had it not been for the incredible courage and bravery of "those that survived" this terrible ordeal...heroes like James and Margret Reed, William McCutchen, and William Eddy...as well as those that were purely motivated by the knowledge of doing a good deed, like John Stark, many more would not have made it. Their story is one of the most valiant tales in human history.

James and Margret Reed's oldest daughter Virginia wrote to her cousin a few months after they had made it to safety. In her letter she wrote..."I have not written to you about half of our trouble. But thank God we have got through. We have left everything, but I don't care for that. We have got through with our lives. I have learned...never take no cut offs and hurry along as fast as you can."

This photo at Alder Creek was taken 30 years after the Donner Party ordeal. The 10-foot tall stumps of trees that were cut for shelter and firewood, indicate how deep the snow was at the time George and Jacob Donner and their families were there.

CHAPTER THIRTY

MODERN DAY TAHOE PIONEERS
Harvey Gross and Bill Harrah

There have been many legendary figures that have helped shape the history of Lake Tahoe. Lucky Baldwin (chapter ten), George Whittell Jr. (chapter twelve), and D.L. Bliss (chapter sixteen) to name just a few. These are characters from Lake Tahoe's "early days," and though their legacies still impact us even today…there are a few larger-than-life figures from Lake Tahoe's more recent times, who have placed their indelible mark on Lake Tahoe history in ways unmatched and unrivaled over the annals of time.

Harvey Gross

Harvey Gross was born in Nebraska in 1905. As a young man he made his way to California, eventually settling in Sacramento. Harvey became involved in the meat business, working his way around as a butcher, a meat packer, and eventually as a wholesaler to restaurants and butcher shops. Harvey met and married Llewellyn Barkley, and the two continued to grow their successful meat wholesale business.

Part of Gross's wholesale business were the restaurants and casinos at fledging South Lake Tahoe and Stateline. Harvey enjoyed the Lake, and the couple would make frequent weekend visits, enjoying Lake Tahoe and spending a little time at some of the small Nevada casinos.

With gas rationing in full affect, the casinos at Lake Tahoe struggled during World War II. Land values dropped. Harvey thought he saw an opportunity, and, in 1944, he and Llewellyn purchased seven acres on Hwy. 50 at Stateline, NV for a great price. They built a small one-room cabin, brought in six slot machines and two card tables, built a lunch counter, and operated the only 24-hour gas pump between Placerville and Carson City. They nailed a wagon wheel above the front door…and Harvey's Wagon Wheel Saloon & Gambling Hall at Lake Tahoe was born.

The Gross' gambling hall did a bang up business during the summer months, but winters were quite different. Snow removal from the highways was still fairly new and ineffective, and snowy roads often hindered travel up to the Lake. Harvey and Llewellyn and their employees (who were also their friends) spent a good deal of the winter sitting around the fireplace and telling stories. One year, Harvey even flooded the parking lot, turning it into an ice rink. But, business during the winter remained poor.

Frustrated by the State of California's inability to keep Hwy. 50 consistently open over Echo Summit, Harvey and a few other South Tahoe business owners donned their winter gear, rolled up their sleeves, and dug out the road at Echo themselves with shovels…just to prove to the State that keeping the road open was possible. Feeling a bit "pressured," Cal-Trans placed a maintenance station at Echo Summit the next year, greatly improving their ability to keep Hwy. 50 open. Winter visitation to South Tahoe...had begun.

All of South Tahoe benefited from its new "year-round" accessibility... including Harvey's Wagon Wheel. Business grew so well that in the early 1960s, Harvey bought more land and moved across the street. He built Tahoe's first high-rise...an 11-story, 197 room hotel/casino and changed the name to Harvey's Resort Hotel & Casino.

Harvey's continued to grow with an additional expansion planned. But that was temporarily interrupted when, in 1980, an extortionist's bomb blew a five-story hole in the hotel tower, causing millions of dollars in damage (see chapter 15). After the proverbial "dust had settled," the expansion moved forward, and, nine months later, Harvey attended the grand opening of his remodeled and repaired hotel/casino.

Harvey passed away in 1983. His daughter and son-in-law continued to operate the Lake Tahoe landmark until 2001. In that year, the longtime competitor across the street- Harrah's, bought out Harvey's. Over the past two decades, ownership at Stateline casinos has changed several times. As of early 2023, Harrah's and Harvey's at Lake Tahoe are both part of the large Caesar's Entertainment Inc.

Harvey Gross's legacy will live forever along the shores of Lake Tahoe. His risk taking, determination, and "can do" spirit helped bring South Tahoe to the forefront of premiere, year round, outdoor destinations, and entertainment.

Harvey Gross was a visionary who saw Lake Tahoe's potential for high stakes gaming.

Harvey's Wagon Wheel opened in 1944 and quickly expanded. It featured the only 24-hour gas pumps between Placerville and Carson City!

Harvey Gross built the first high rise at Lake Tahoe in the early 1960s.

William Harrah

William Harrah was one the world's best known and most successful casino operators. Innovative and creative, his powerful influence in the gaming industry can still be seen today. He was a force to be reckoned with…even after he passed.

Born in South Pasadena, California in 1911, Bill Harrah learned much from his attorney father John, who specialized in providing legal advice to bootleggers. John Harrah also dabbled in politics and other small businesses. John taught Bill the power of strong will and determination, skills that helped him for the rest of his life.

Bill enrolled in UCLA's Medical Engineering Department but had to drop out as the Great Depression set in. Bill worked and helped in his family's various small businesses, including a pool hall, shooting gallery, and a bingo-style operation known as the "Reno Game." Gambling in California was illegal at that time, but games of skill based on bingo were allowed. The Reno Game operated with thirty-three players rolling small balls down a ramp, which had various marked slots cut into it. The first player to match a four-card suit would win. However…John often used shills in his games.

Law enforcement didn't look kindly upon the operation and closed it down several times. But Bill's father was a smart attorney, and always got their permit to operate the games reinstated. Displeased with the continual run ins with the law, Bill advised his father to get rid of the shills and invest more in the business. His father agreed and told Bill to take over running the games. Bill was only 21 when he became the manager of his first "gaming" operation. Bill did well, grossing as much as $50,000 a year.

Gambling had become legal in Nevada at about this same time. On a visit to Reno in the early 1930s, Bill saw the free and easy way gaming was operated in the Silver State. Tired of the restricted laws of California, he opened his first Reno bingo club in October of 1937. The Reno gaming business was already dominated by much larger (and powerful) operators like Jim McKay, Nick Abelman, and Bill Graham, and Harrah's new club did miserably. He had to close down in just 17 days.

Bill Harrah (R) at his Bingo Hall in Reno- 1950s- with his father John Harrah.

Not to be deterred, he found a partner to back him in another attempt. Bill opened the "Harrah's Plaza Tango" followed shortly by the "Tango Club." Both bingo clubs were located close to Reno's main gaming action. The new clubs did better, but still were not producing the action he needed.

Through his father's business dealings in Southern California, Bill had a contact in Reno...a respected ex-bootlegger Cal Custer. Cal had "juice" with most of the major gaming men in town. He "stood up" for young Bill, and Harrah was eventually admitted into the fraternity of Reno big time operators. Business began to slowly improve in his bingo clubs.

In 1940, Bill had done well enough to open a bigger club in Reno he named Harrah's Reno. He emphasized exceptional customer service and attention to detail from his employees...and it paid off. Harrah's Reno became renowned for its friendly and professional staff.

In 1955, Bill bought the Gateway Club at Stateline, Nevada. The Gateway was a bit dingy, being housed in a Quonset hut. Bill built a false front around it, did some interior remodeling and renamed it Harrah's Club at South Shore Lake Tahoe, and brought in the same great quality of service his operations had become known for. Four years later, he relocated across the highway, in what at the time became the largest single structure in the world devoted to gaming.

Bill Harrah bought the old Gateway Club, remodeled it, and opened his first Lake Tahoe casino in 1955.

It was also in 1955, that Bill used his influence with the State of Nevada to have the Nevada Gaming Control Board established to regulate and oversee gaming in the state.

The Lake Tahoe casino did well...during the warmer months. But, when winter set in and the roads became difficult, business dried up. First, Bill contributed several snowplows at his own expense to help keep the Lake Tahoe wintery roads open. Then, Bill Harrah came up with an idea that revolutionized the gaming business throughout Nevada. He established an extensive bus network, which provided free transportation (and usually lunch) to customers from 31 different California cities to his gaming club. He even opened a childcare for gaming parents to drop off their youngins'.

Bill was the first casino owner to open his doors to people of all races and colors. He hired anyone who was fit for the job, looking past the color and sex of the individual. He hired some of the first women 21 dealers in Nevada.

Things continued to go right for Bill Harrah. By 1961, his casinos were the second largest employer in Nevada. He built a 24-story hotel in Reno in 1968, and a 17-story hotel at Lake Tahoe in 1973. His management style caused a gaming analyst to declare, "Harrah's is the most tightly controlled and best managed casino company in the world." He took his company public, and, in 1973, became the first casino company to be listed on the New York Stock Exchange. Also in 1973, he expanded into the Las Vegas market, becoming the first gaming company to operate casinos in three different locations.

Bill loved cars. As he became wealthier, he turned his interest to acquiring some of the rarest automobiles on the planet. He displayed them for public enjoyment at his own museum he had built in Reno.

William Harrah passed away in 1978. Since that time, the company has changed hands a few times, and is now (2023) part of the Caesar's Entertainment group...the largest casino operator in the world.

Some may argue that Lake Tahoe would be "better off" without the development it has experienced due to gaming. But there is no doubt that thanks to visionaries like Bill Harrah and Harvey Gross, Lake Tahoe became much better known...and created thousands of new admirers...and supporters... of this beautiful mountain lake and the many pleasures it has to offer.

Harrah's has been an institution at Lake Tahoe for almost 70-years.

CHAPTER THIRTY-ONE

SUMMER CAMP MEMORIES
South Tahoe's Camp Chonokis

Not all old historic properties of Lake Tahoe's bygone era are well known. There are a few secret gems that catered to specialized groups and escaped the notoriety their more popular neighbors attained. But that isn't to say the memories and experiences they created are not as valued by its alumni than any other. In fact…far from it.

In the mid-1920s, Mabel Winter (later she became Mabel Whitney) and Ethel Pope had an idea that young women should have the opportunity to spend time in the mountains, enjoying the great outdoors, and learning important life skills. Together, they purchased twenty acres of land near the California/Nevada state line, about one-half mile from South Lake Tahoe's shore. They named their new summer retreat for girls…Camp Chonokis.

The word Chonokis was reportedly from the Washo dialect, meaning Sugar Pine. The property was said to have had several beautiful specimens of this king of pines that somehow had escaped the lumberman's ax.

Both Winter-Whitney and Pope were school teachers. They shared the common notion that a less structured outdoor learning experience would make a great offering for young women who attended a regimented academic program during their school year. Winter-Whitney and Pope's plan was to offer a six-week summer camp program in the enchanting outdoors of Lake Tahoe. After only one year, Pope sold her interest in Camp Chonokis to Winter.

In the first full season of 1928, the camp hosted twelve campers. The six camp counselors were mostly teachers from San Francisco. The ability to handle more campers grew. By 1952, the last summer Winter-Whitney was involved in its operation, Camp Chonokis hosted 35 young women. When it first opened in 1928, the fee for a six-week session was $275.00. Twenty-four years later, it had increased to $425.00. A few years after opening, Camp Chonokis also offered a shortened two-week winter camp during Christmas vacation. During World War Two, at the government's urging, the camp offered a second shorter session so as to allow more young women the chance to leave their urban environs during this stressful wartime period.

Camp Chonokis occupied twenty acres of mostly forested and level Tahoe Basin. There was a main lodge, shower house, and tent cabins. In the early 1930s, Winter-Whitney had a log house built. She named it Tyschina, a Russian word meaning peace or calm. She planned for the cabin to be her home after she retired someday. When the girls were in camp, the log building was used for reading, music, and meetings.

What would a summer camp be without horseback riding? This was one of the most popular of all camp activities. The camp even put together a rodeo for the young women held towards the end of their session. Drama, hiking, choir, dancing, and water sports rounded out the summer activities. At the end of the six weeks, the camp put on an "open air theatre," and invited parents and local South Tahoe residents to come watch the girls perform.

One of the most enduring traditions of the camp was the adoption of nicknames for staff and campers. Winter-Whitney was known as "Bliz," short for Blizzard. Mugs, G3, Pinesap, and Pinecone were a few other monikers affectionately bantered about.

Camp Chonokis campers learning the fine art of canoe rowing...on dry land.

Winter met and married Robert Whitney in the late 1940s. Her new life made it more difficult to continue with Camp Chonokis. In 1953, she leased the camp to a former Chonokis camper and counselor. Costs and logistics proved just too difficult for the new operator, and the camp never reopened after that summer. Winter-Whitney and her husband would use the log cabin as a summer vacation home for the next few years…but its time as a memory making summer camp came to an end.

A few of the girls would arrive by train to Tahoe City, and take the steamer across the Lake to Camp Chonokis on Tahoe's south shore.

Summers at Camp Chonokis were always remembered with special sentiment by all who attended and worked at the camp. One of Camp Chonokis' most treasured traditions was the compilation of poems and prose from campers and staff entered into the yearly "Chonokis Logs." These, plus the photograph albums for each camp season, attest to the enthusiasm with which campers hiked, swam, rode, and played among the Sugar Pines. The property is now owned by the U.S. Forest Service. Nothing really remains of the old place, except the faded photos in scrapbooks, and the many lifelong memories of young women…and their time well spent in the mountains at magical Lake Tahoe.

Camp Chonokis girls on a hike in what has become Desolation Wilderness.

It just wouldn't be summer camp if there was no canoeing.
Out on a choppy Lake Tahoe.

CHAPTER THIRTY-TWO

DAT-SO-LA-LEE
The Greatest Lake Tahoe Artist

Tales Along
LAKE TAHOE SHORES

Lake Tahoe has been the home and inspiration of a number of very skilled artists and crafts-persons over the years. This alpine mountain gem brings out the best in many. Washo tribal member Dat-So-La-Lee is arguably the "best" and most talented artisan to have called Lake Tahoe home.

Picture a tranquil Lake Tahoe scene, of a small house bordering a lush meadow, with a Native American woman meticulously but easily weaving a beautiful basket out of strips of willow. Her name was Dat-So-La-Lee.

Dat-So-La-Lee's given name at birth was Dabuda, which prophetically translates to "Young Willow." She was born in the Carson Valley at the base of the Sierra Nevada Mountains around 1829. Like all her Washo neighbors, her family would move between the Carson Valley in the winters to the shores of Lake Tahoe in the summer. As a child, she watched tribal elders weave utility baskets for a variety of uses ranging from carrying pine nuts to a vessel for water. She learned how to rip the willow into strips and make an assortment of dyes from tree bark, roots, and other substances.

As a young woman, Dat-So-La-Lee worked as a domestic for miners in Alpine County, California during the silver boom of the 1870s. In 1888, she took the "legal" name of Louisa Keyser, as she and her husband Charlie lived and worked at Charlie Keyser's Carson Valley ranch.

Dat-So-La-Lee made woven baskets and bottles throughout her adolescence and young adult years. During Lake Tahoe's summer tourist season, she would join with other Washo women to sell her handmade work to visitors and tourists. In 1895, Carson City/Lake Tahoe business owners Abe and Amy Cohn stopped by the Washo's Lake Tahoe site to look at their work. The Cohn's were very impressed by Dat-So-La-Lee's beautiful hand-woven works with their intricate designs. They bought several of her pieces and resold them in their Lake Tahoe curio shop for a nice profit.

The Cohns came back to see Dat-So-La-Lee. They offered her and her husband a small house to live in at Lake Tahoe (summers) and Carson City (winters) and also offered to take care of most of their living expenses. In return, the Cohns would receive all of Dat-So-La-Lee's basketry to sell at their Lake Tahoe and Carson City shops. She agreed, and the arrangement provided a comfortable, if not affluent, life for her and her husband.

Dat-So-La-Lee's skills continued to develop, and her baskets became highly prized and sought after. Cohn's customer would pay top dollar for her work. The Cohns would take her to art shows throughout California, and she gained a bit of celebrity status. Dat-So-La-Lee never learned to write, and "signed" the bill of sales certifying authenticity, with her handprint.

Her preferred style of weaving became known as "day-gee-coop." She would start with a small circular base, with the basket extending upwards and out to a maximum circumference, then narrowing the opening to approximately the same size as the base.

The Cohn's made up names and fabricated stories around her baskets to promote their sale to collectors. Names such as "Our People Used Magic Arrows," "Bright Morning Lights," "The Chief's Compact," and "Going to War" were given to what in reality was commissioned artwork.

Cohn kept detailed records of Dat-So-La-Lee's work. He recorded in a ledger a description of the basket, stitches to the inch, the design, and the time involved in its fabrication. Some of her baskets were so intricate and complex, they took her months to complete. Each piece of her work was unique and perfect in symmetry and design.

As the years went by, the eyestrain caused by years of detailed basket weaving began to take its toll and caused Dat-So-La-Lee's vision to fail. It is said for the last years of her life, she worked her weaving magic in the dark. She had become so expert at weaving her intricate designs that she could do so without seeing. Dat-So-La-Lee passed away in 1925 and is buried at the Stewart Indian Cemetery near Carson City.

Some historians estimate Dat-So-La-Lee produced about 300 handmade pieces during her lifetime, with 120 being documented from 1895 to 1925 by the Cohns. Her stunning work is at several museums in Nevada, and at the Gatekeeper's Museum in Tahoe City. Her work is of such high regard it is also on display at the Penn Museum in Philadelphia, the Smithsonian National Museum of the American Indian in Washington D.C., and the Metropolitan Museum of Art in New York.

Dat-So-La-Lee memories and visions were beautifully woven into her baskets, and her legacy lives on to remind us of the history and unique tribal artistry of the Washo people.

Dat-So-La-Lee at Lake Tahoe displaying some of her artistry.

Washo Dat-So-La-Lee was one of the finest basket makers to have ever lived.

Dat-So-La-Lee's baskets were perfect pieces of symmetry.

Abe and Amy (seated) Cohn sold Dat-So-La-Lee's and other
Native American's baskets at their Tahoe City and Carson City curio shops.

Dah-So-La-Lee created intricate bottles and other woven masterpieces,
as well as her famous baskets.

CHAPTER THIRTY-THREE

LIGHTS, CAMERA, ACTION!
Lake Tahoe at the Movies

The dramatic landscape of Lake Tahoe and the surrounding area has been a favorite backdrop for many Hollywood producers and directors over the years. The expansive shimmering blue lake, the deep rich emerald forests, and the brooding snow capped peaks, provide a perfect setting for scenes ranging from an outdoor recreation mecca to a romantic interlude.

Its diverse scenery and relatively close proximity to Hollywood caused Lake Tahoe to find a place in feature films shortly after the first motion pictures appeared on the silver screen.

In 1925, Charlie Chaplin brought a cast of hundreds to the mountains near Donner Pass to film his epic, *The Gold Rush*. Chaplin starred, produced, and directed the film. In it, he emphasized the lengths people went to achieve fortune and romance…while at the same time settling the American West. The classic led some to say it was the greatest film from the silent era.

Nelson Eddy sang one of our favorite old time classic ballads, "Indian Love Call" (of Yosemite Firefall fame) to Jeanette MacDonald with Lake Tahoe mountains in the background in the 1936 romantic musical, *Rose Marie*. The movie also features "all American good guy" Jimmy Stewart as a murderer-bad guy, while the director plays up the movie's melodramatic aspects for laughs. There are several other shots of Big Blue in this tinsel town classic.

During the peak of Hollywood's film noir era of the 1940s and '50s, powerhouse Robert Mitchum plays a small-town gas station owner who can't escape his shady past in *Out of the Past*. Kirk Douglas plays the campy yet rich antagonist. The movie features dramatic shots of Emerald Bay, as well as the Bridgeport Valley at the base of the High Sierra on Hwy. 395.

A Place in the Sun- 1951, won six Academy Awards and was nominated for three more. The riveting drama about class struggle features Montgomery Cliff and Shelly Winters at their best, and a fledging 17-year old Elizabeth Taylor playing in her first adult role. The movie has many memorable Lake Tahoe scenes including Cliff towing a water-skiing Taylor in a classic wooden boat across a placid Lake Tahoe on a beautiful Sierra summer day.

Anyone who has seen the time honored *The Godfather Part II* will associate some of the most iconic scenes in Hollywood movie making with Lake Tahoe. Situated near Homewood on Tahoe's west shore, Fleur du Lac Estate is a home originally built by steel magnate Henry Kaiser in 1938. The home was the setting where Michael Corleone put on his son's first communion celebration, and the backdrop for Fredo Corleone's death at the hands of Al Neri, after Neri takes him out on Lake Tahoe to fish.

Harrison Ford brought the Indiana Jones franchise to the Lake Tahoe area in 1984. Though no scenes were actually filmed at the Lake, just over the hill, the American River Canyon substituted for the Himalayas. Ford and his sidekick Short Round navigate some intense rapids that are partly shot on the American River.

In 1992, Kevin Costner and Whitney Houston spent time at Lake Tahoe filming scenes for *The Bodyguard*. A beautiful estate at Fallen Leaf Lake known as the Tallac House served as the location for the lake house sequences, including the famous scene where Frank (Costner) dove into the icy cold water to save Fletcher's (Houston) son.

2022 saw the release of *Top Gun: Maverick,* the highest grossing film of that year starring the legendary Tom Cruise. Some of the aerial dogfight scenes were shot above the Sierra Nevada by Lake Tahoe; a parachuting scene was filmed at Washoe Meadows State Park, and the scene where Maverick tries to escape from an airport is none other than the Lake Tahoe Airport at South Lake Tahoe.

There are dozens of other feature films that have a Tahoe scene or two appear. Some of the more recent include *Smokin' Aces, Survivors, Bad Times at the El Royale, Into the Wild, Misery,* and *Cobb*, to name just a few. In addition, hundreds of television shows, commercials, and shorts have also used the majestic Lake Tahoe scenery.

Undoubtedly there will be more Hollywood directors and producers that seek out the spectacular scenery of Lake Tahoe to appear in their films in the future. The many successful productions over the years demonstrate that location scouts will continue to pursue the Lake Tahoe area's unmatched scenic quality as an ideal cinematography backdrop as long as films are being made.

Nelson Eddy serenades Jeannette MacDonald while canoeing across Lake Tahoe in the 1930s Hollywood classic, *Rose Marie.*

Charlie Chaplin (bottom L) brought in a cast of hundreds, to film this legendary shot from the *Klondike Gold Rush*...near Truckee in 1925.

Fredo Corleone goes on his last fishing trip, with Al Neri on Lake Tahoe in *The Godfather Part II*.

MORE
LAKE TAHOE HISTORY?

Lake Tahoe Historical Society and Museum
3058 Lake Tahoe Blvd., South Lake Tahoe, CA 96150
(530) 541-5458 | http://www.laketahoemuseum.org

Tallac Historic Site
1 Heritage Way, South Lake Tahoe, CA 96150
(530) 544-7383 | info@tahoeheritage.org

Thunderbird Lodge, George Whittell Estate Tours
Shuttles leave from the Incline Village Visitors Center,
969 Tahoe Blvd., Incline Village, NV 89451 | For tours-(800) 468-2463
https://thunderbirdtahoe.org

Gatekeeper's Museum- North Lake Tahoe Historical Society
130 West Lake Blvd., Tahoe City, CA 96145
(530) 583-1762 | info@northtahoemuseums.org

Tahoe Maritime Museum
401 W. Lake Blvd.,Tahoe City, CA 96145
(530) 583-9283 | https://www.facebook.com/TahoeMaritimeMuseum

Hellman-Ehrman Mansion- Ed Z-berg Sugar Pine Point State Park
7360 W. Lake Blvd., Tahoma, CA 96142
(530) 525-9528 | https://www.parks.ca.gov/?page_id=991

Vikingsholm- Emerald Bay State Park
CA Hwy. 89, Emerald Bay, CA 96142
(530) 583-9911 | https://sierrastateparks.org/emerald-bay-state-park/viking-sholm-tours

Note- Most museums are closed or have limited hours during the winter months. Be sure and call ahead before you plan your visit.

Image by Leslie Engelhart. Leslie Engelhart Western Art; http://www.cow-boyprints.com/

Tales Along
LAKE TAHOE SHORES

CHAPTER THIRTY-FOUR

ALL ABOARD!
Railroading at Lake Tahoe

The Lake Tahoe Basin seems an unlikely spot for a train. The grade up from the Washoe, Eagle, and Carson Valleys is prohibitively steep to construct a workable railroad grade. It was difficult enough to build a wagon road over Echo Summit (formerly Johnson's Pass), much less lay a rail line down the steep and precipitous slope. But Lake Tahoe has indeed been home to at least five railroads (three for logging, two for passenger service) during its place in time, and evidence of a few of them is still visible today.

Carson and Tahoe Lumber and Fluming Company Railroad

Lake Tahoe's abject history of deforestation was well under way by the mid-1860s, as sawmills, constructed at the natural harbor at Glenbrook, were milling the Lake's trees. At first the sawed logs were hauled up Glenbrook Canyon to Summit (now Spooner Summit), and then steeply down the Clear Creek grade to Carson City and eventually the Comstock. The painstakingly slow trip was accomplished by lumber wagons pulled by oxen.

The demand for lumber grew, as did Glenbrook. More sawmills, bunkhouses, hotels, telegraph offices, and businesses sprang up. Steamers were brought in to provide guests with easy transit to Tahoe City and the stage line.

By the early 1870s, D.L. Bliss and other wealthy investors from the Comstock arrived at Glenbrook and purchased much of the existing logging operation. A V-flume (see chapter thirteen) was constructed down Clear Creek Canyon, greatly speeding the delivery of timber down to Carson City. But getting the wood 920-feet up by oxen to the beginning of the flume at the summit was still interminably slow.

In 1874, Bliss and his Carson and Tahoe Lumber and Fluming Company constructed an 8.75-mile narrow gauge rail line up from Glenbrook to the beginning of the V-flume at Spooner Summit. Its sole purpose was to haul lumber and cordwood. Ten trestles and a 270-foot-long tunnel were rapidly constructed by four crews of Chinese laborers, who probably were veterans of building the transcontinental railroad in the 1860s.

Bliss purchased two little but powerful Baldwin locomotives for his new line. Each engine could pull 70 tons of wood on 5 or 6 cars, up the 2.44% grade at a speedy 10-MPH. The brilliantly engineered rail line operated for 23 years, greatly adding to the efficient harvesting of Lake Tahoe's timber.

Lake Valley Railroad

By the 1880s, the cry for more wood for the Comstock was louder than ever. South Tahoe resident George Chubbuck thought he saw an opportunity to cash in on the demand for Tahoe trees. He purchased 1,200 acres of forested land in the vicinity of what is now Sierra House, South Tahoe. He contracted with D.L. Bliss to provide a set amount of wood and went to work laying out his rail line. But his venture was in trouble from the start.

At first, Chubbuck used "wooden" track faced with scrap iron. His line extended 4 ½-miles into the Tahoe forests, and oxen were cumbersomely used to pull the rail cars of wood to the lake shore. In an attempt to improve the operations, Chubbuck purchased an old steam locomotive to replace the oxen. But the vintage engine was too heavy for the wooden rails. Cars became unstable and uneven, and the operation was fraught with breakdowns.

Unable to meet the obligation of his contract, Chubbuck was forced into bankruptcy, and Bliss took over the line in 1886. Bliss purchased thousands of additional acres of South Tahoe forests and went to work. He replaced the wooden rails with iron, extended the line to over seven miles (eventually 11 ½), brought in two steam narrow gauge locomotives, and built an 1,800-foot pier into Lake Tahoe at Bijou to unload his lumber for barging.

Bliss' operation worked well...for a few years. By 1890, silver mining in the Comstock was declining steeply, and the demand for Tahoe lumber dried up...but not before tens of millions of board feet of South Tahoe timber were cut and harvested. In 1898, the Lake Valley Railroad came to an end.

Sierra Nevada Wood & Lumber Company Railroad

At the northeast corner of Lake Tahoe sits Sand Harbor. The famous Incline Tramway (chapter twenty-three) hauled lumber 1,400' up the steep Lake Tahoe mountainside to a tunnel/flume that carried the wood down to Washoe Valley and on to the Comstock. But getting the cut trees to the sawmills near Sand Harbor required the effort of another Lake Tahoe rail line.

Walter Hobart and his Sierra Nevada Wood & Lumber Company leveled a railbed and laid track two miles south into the Tahoe woods, and another rail line two miles west towards Crystal Bay. The two extensions greatly increased the amount of Tahoe forests Hobart could harvest and bring into his Sand Harbor mill.

Like Chubbuck on the South Shore, Hobart eventually sold his entire operation to D.L. Bliss. The logging and little rail line continued for a few more years, before steaming to an end.

Lake Tahoe Railroad

As the great Comstock silver boom came to an end in the 1890s, D.L. Bliss, who had made a fortune providing lumber from Lake Tahoe's forests to the mining towns of Virginia City and Gold Hill, was looking for new opportunities. Though the trees were mostly gone, magnificent Lake Tahoe itself remained, and Bliss thought tourists would come if faster and more comfortable transportation could be provided.

Bliss had already operated resort hotels at Glenbrook, and so he set out in 1898 to build a new resort on property he owned near Tahoe City. His plan was to build a new rail line that would connect with the main Southern Pacific Railroad line at Truckee, 16 miles along the Truckee River Canyon. Tourists would be able to take a train from almost any spot in the United

States direct to Lake Tahoe at Tahoe City. Bliss would build his Tahoe Tavern, a 225-room luxury hotel catering to the arriving tourists at Tahoe City.

Bliss had most of the track from his Glenbrook, South Tahoe, and Incline logging railroads pulled up and barged to Tahoe City, to build his new passenger service line. He barged a few of his logging locomotives over to Tahoe City as well. The narrow gauge to Truckee was completed, and the Tahoe Tavern opened. Serious tourism had arrived at Lake Tahoe.

The Southern Pacific bought Bliss' Lake Tahoe Railroad in 1925 and converted it into a standard gauge line. But, as highways improved and autos became more reliable, visitors to Lake Tahoe began arriving by their cars in greater and greater numbers. In 1943, added to by the outbreak of World War Two, transport to Lake Tahoe by train…came to an end.

The track was taken up and sold for scrap, but the railroad grade was eventually turned into a bike/walking path…and has become a true Lake Tahoe treasure. In addition, for those history buffs that enjoy visiting locations of Lake Tahoe's historic past, the railroad grade of the old Lake Valley Railroad at South Lake Tahoe is also clearly seen in a few places near Pioneer Trail.

Carson and Tahoe Lumber and Fluming Company Railroad at Glenbrook, required ten wooden trestles and a 270' long tunnel to make its way almost nine miles to Spooner Summit.

Tahoe, Trout Creek & Pacific Railroad (TTC & PR)

The TTC & PR was strictly a narrow gauge, tourist train that operated at South Lake Tahoe in 1970 and '71. Tracks were laid right on the dirt without proper grading and gravel. Running from Al Tahoe to near Pioneer Trail, the owners had plans to develop it into a "resort transportation system," extending the line to "ski areas, campgrounds, and other local recreation sites."

The locomotives were bought from the Hawaii Railway sugar plantation,

141

and guests would ride in an open air converted ore car. Looking at their brochures, the rail line put a great emphasis on customer service, but the grand plans to expand and extend the short line never materialized. The TTC & PR only operated in 1970 and '71, and then steamed off to a distant depot.

The Lake Tahoe lumber railroads kept being extended deeper and deeper into the Lake Tahoe forests to obtain the valuable trees for the Comstock.

D.L. Bliss built his Lake Tahoe Railway along the Truckee River Canyon between Truckee and Tahoe City. Today the old grade is a delightful walking/biking path.

EPILOGUE

This brings us to the conclusion of this assemblage of Lake Tahoe history tales. It has been a sheer delight for us to share them with you, and we thank you for allowing us to do so.

The human history of a place can be complex, unusual, and, at times, confusing. The Lake Tahoe region is no exception. Reflecting back on how this finest of Mother Nature's temples has evolved from a quiet peaceful sanctuary for an ancient culture…to a natural resource that helped fuel one of the most significant industrializations the world has known…to its eminent position as a cathedral of recreation and rejuvenation for millions…to being in danger of being "loved to death"…certainly causes us to pause and ponder…what will be the fate for Lake Tahoe in the years ahead.

We find ourselves grateful for those who have gone before and have smoothed a path for us at this alpine mountain gem. And we are reminded, we all stand on and benefit in varying ways, from the hard work of those who have forged a way before us.

Many will come to visit or live at Lake Tahoe in the years ahead. We are certainly not the last to walk Lake Tahoe trails, glide across its waters, witness its inspiring views, or experience its spiritual powers. While we are thankful for the foundations of those who have gone before, we also sense an important obligation to those who will come after us…to leave Lake Tahoe…and the earth in a better condition than we found it.

We live in the present…and plan and worry for the future. Everything that has been done is "history," meaning that history directly affects us every day. History spans all cultures, eras, and environments; it is an immovable factor that can be called upon for knowledge and insight into how we got to this point we are at now…and how things will continue to develop in the future.

President Theodore Roosevelt is quoted as having said, "It is only by knowing about our past…that we can be prepared to meet our future." We cannot agree more with our 26th Chief Executive. While we tried to share anecdotes of Lake Tahoe history we found not only interesting…but hopefully, in some cases, amusing…we also hope that knowing and understanding these tales from Lake Tahoe's storied past will make us all…even in a small way…better prepared to help Lake Tahoe "live its best life" in the future as well.

Nature is an inspirational source for us human beings. Albert Einstein once said, "We know less than one thousandth of one percent of what nature has to reveal to us." We hope to continue to learn what nature will reveal. Enjoying nature - whether it be at Lake Tahoe, on the coast at Big Sur, walking through a grove of Giant Sequoias, or at any other magical place we experience - can cleanse our minds, clear our thinking, and richly inspire us.

Inspiration is everywhere. If we grab that spark of it for ourselves…we can also use it to inspire others. From watching the sun shine its first morning light on Mt. Tallac, to enjoying the melody of a Sierra storm as it passes through the Jeffrey Pines…Lake Tahoe often provides us with a powerful, inspirational moment. And with inspiration…we can affect our future. If we think and act as if what we do can make a difference, then it shall surely be so. The small steps we take…will bring about the most lasting change.

Thank you all for being part of this grand family that loves and respects….and hopes and plans for the best for Lake Tahoe. Big Blue has a very special place in our hearts…and we know that it does for you too. We encourage you to create your own *Tales Along Lake Tahoe Shores*, that provide you with special lifetime memories…and to be a beacon of inspiring light for all those to come.

For the love and inspiration of *Big Blue*, *David & Gayle Woodruff*

**Ms. Irene Meyn (photographer) waving goodbye to the
S.S. Tahoe as it leaves the Al Tahoe Pier- circa 1913.**

144

SELECTED BIBLIOGRAPHY

Ch. 1- *WA SHE SHU: "The Washoe People" Past and Present;* The Washoe Tribe of California and Nevada- Washoe Cultural Resource Office

Ch. 2- City of South Lake Tahoe- Airports history, *The Record-Courier,* www.tahoetopia.com, www.newspapers.com; *Reno Gazette Journal*

Ch. 3- *The Saga of Lake Tahoe Volumes 1 and 2;* E.B. Scott, U.S. Forest Service

Ch. 4- www.tahoemagazine.com; Mark McLaughlin, www.en.wikipedia.org, laketahoenews.net, https://www.keeptahoeblue.org

Ch. 5- www.en.wikipedia.org, www.imdb.com, www.bonanza,fandom. com, www.metv.com, *Tahoe Beneath the Surface;* Scott Lankford

Ch. 6- *The Saga of Lake Tahoe Volume 1;* E.B. Scott, *Tahoe Daily Tribune;* Amanda Fehd, www.tahoetopia.com

Ch. 7- www.en.wikipedia.org, www.fbi.gov, The Grand Scheme podcast-Wondry; John Stamos, *Reno Gazette Journal*; Bob Thomas and Warren Lerude, https://www.pausatf.org/data/2013/tfechosummit.html

Ch. 8- *Tahoe Magazine;* Tim Hauserman, www.en.wikipedia.org, www. usda.org, *Tahoe Quarterly;* Sylas Wright

Ch. 9- *Echo Summit;* Paul DeWitt and Dorothy De Mare, www.eid.org, Echo Lakes Association Records

Ch.10- www.en.wikipedia.org, KCET Public Television; *Elias 'Lucky' Baldwin: Land Baron of Southern California*, www.arcadia.gov, Lake Tahoe Historical Society Newsletters; June 1989 and Winter 2008

Ch.11- www.en.wikipedia.com, *The Saga of Lake Tahoe Volume 1*; E.B. Scott, www.legendsofamerica.com, NevadaNewsGroup; Dennis Cassinelli, www. ponyexpress.com

Ch.12- www.thunderbird.org, www.autoweek.com, *Castle in the Sky*; Ronald and Susan James, *The Saga of Lake Tahoe Volume 1*; E.B. Scott

Ch. 13- *Sierra Sun;* Judy DuPuy, *Nevada Magazine;* Bob Sagan

Ch. 14- Lake Tahoe Historical Society Newsletters; May 1991, June 1991, Fall 2003, www.tahoeculture.com, *The Saga of Lake Tahoe Volume 1*; E.B. Scott

Ch. 15- *The Atavist Magazine;* Adam Higginbotham, FBI Archives; The Case of the Harvey's Casino Bomb, *Tahoe Quarterly Magazine*; Matthew Renda

Ch. 16- https://en.wikipedia.org/, https://foresthistory.org, https://www. kunr.org/, Lake Tahoe Historical Society Newsletter; Summer 2003

Ch. 17- https://www.leg.state.nv.us, *The Saga of Lake Tahoe Volume 1*; E.B. Scott, https://www.clairitage.com; Karen Dustman

Ch. 18- *John A. Snowshoe Thompson, Pioneer Mail Carrier of the Sierra*; Frank Tortorich, https://thestormking.com/

Ch. 19- www.stewartindianschool.com, *Sierra Nevada Ally*; Kelsey Penrose, *A History of the Stewart Indian School;* Bonnie Thompson, *Solano Daily Republic*; Susan Winlow

Ch. 20- *Tahoe Daily Tribune*; Amanda Fehd, *Tahoe Beneath the Surface*; Scott Lankford, Monterey County Historical Society

Ch. 21- http://southtahoenow.com/story/11/12/2013/; Paula Peterson, Lake Tahoe Historical Society Newsletters; Winter 2002 and Winter 2006, *Tahoe Magazine*; Mark McLaughlin

Ch. 22- Lake Tahoe Historical Society Newsletter; Winter 1991, *Reno Gazette Journal, Tahoe Daily Tribune;* Jeremy Evans, *Forbes Magazine*; Michael Alpiner, https://www.skiheavenly.com,https://snowbrains.com/the-history-of-skiing-lake-tahoe

Ch. 23- *The Saga of Lake Tahoe Volumes 1 and 2*; E.B. Scott, https://www.truckeehistory.org/sierra-nevada-wood-and-lumber-company.html

Ch. 24- *The Saga of Lake Tahoe Volume 1*; E.B. Scott, Explore Reno-Tahoe, Lake Tahoe, *A Maritime History*; Peter Goin, Lake Tahoe Historical Society Newsletter; Fall 2002, *Tahoe Quarterly*; Allison Bender

Ch. 25- *Nevada Magazine*; Brandon Wilding, *Hank Monk and Horace Greeley*; Richard Lillard, *True West Magazine*; Brandon Hays, Lake Tahoe Historical Society Newsletters; Winter 1996 and Spring 1998

Ch. 26- *Classic Trains Magazine, Reno Gazette Journal,* Donner Summit Historical Society, https://www.historylink.org/File/5127, *The Seattle Star*

Ch. 27- U.S. Bureau of Reclamation, *Putting California on the Map: Von Schmidt Lines*; David Carle, *Sierra Sun*; Claire McArthur, *Saga of Lake Tahoe Volumes 1 and 2*; E.B. Scott, JSTOR-*Conflict Over Conservation*; Donald J. Pasini, JSTOR-*Why Shouldn't California Have the Grandest Aqueduct in the World?*; Donald J. Pasini, *Tahoe Quarterly*; Matthew Renda

Ch. 28- *Saga of Lake Tahoe Volumes 1 and 2*; E.B. Scott

Ch. 29- *All We Left Behind*; Virginia Reed, www.britannica.com, www.history.com, *History of the Donner Party*; C.F McGlashan, The Academy of Pacific Coast History- *The Patrick Breen Diary*; Patrick Breen

Ch. 30- *Tahoe Daily Tribune*; Rick Chandler, www.fundinguniverse.com, *Forbes Magazine*; Lisa Gubernick, Gaming Library UNLV, www.casinorankings.com, www.nevadagaminghistory.com, *Reno Gazette-Journal*; Siobhan McAndrew

Ch 31- https://archive.library.unr.edu/public/repositories/2/resources/36

Ch. 32- https://nevadawomen.org/research-center/biographies-alphabetical/ dat-so-la-lee/, https://basketweaving.com/shopsite_sc/store/html/dat-so-la-lee.html, https://americanindian.si.edu/exhibitions/infinityofnations/ california-greatbasin/118261.html, https://www.palomar.edu/users/ddozier/ datsolalee.html, *Nevada Appeal*; Brad Horn, *Dat-So-La-Lee, Washo Indian Basketmaker*; Dixie Westergard

Ch. 33- https://www.imdb.com/search/title/?locations=Lake+Tahoe%2C+California%2C+USA, *Tahoe Magazine*; Matthew Renda, *Tahoe Daily Tribune*; Autumn Whitney

Ch. 34- *Saga of Lake Tahoe Volumes 1 and 2*; E.B. Scott, https://www.abandonedrails.com/lake-tahoe-branch, *Sierra Sun*; Gordon Richards

May you always enjoy the tales you create from your own travels...
Along Lake Tahoe Shores.

PHOTO CREDITS

Front Cover-Union Pacific Systems
Back Cover-Southern Pacific Railroad
iii-United States Geological Service
vi-University of Nevada, Reno; Online Digital Collections
viii-California State Archives
x-University of Nevada, Reno; Online Digital Collections
4a & 4b-University of Nevada, Reno; Online Digital Collections
6a & 6b-City of South Lake Tahoe
8-Santa Clarita Historical Society
9-University of Nevada, Reno; Online Digital Collections
10a & 10b-University of Nevada, Reno; Online Digital Collections
12-Newspapers.com; *Reno-Gazette Journal*
13-California Department of Transportation
14a-University of Nevada, Reno; Online Digital Collections
14b-University of Nevada, Reno; Online Digital Collections; Putnam & Valentine
17-fanart.tv
18a-IMDb
18b-Author's Collection
19a-Business Insider
19b-Author's Collection
20a and 20b-Author's Collection
23a and 23b-California State Library
25-newspapers.com; *Reno Gazette-Journal*
26 newspapers.com; *San Francisco Examiner*
28-newspapers.com; *Baltimore Sun*
29-University of Nevada, Reno; Online Digital Collections
30-newspapers.com; R*eno Gazette-Journal*
31 & 32-City of South Lake Tahoe
34a-University of Nevada, Reno; Online Digital Collections
34b-United States Geological Survey
37-Wikipdeia
38a-University of Nevada, Reno; Online Digital Collections
38b-Tahoe Heritage Foundation
40-Author's Collection
41-Pony Express National Museum
42-Society of California Pioneers
44-Thunderbird Lake Tahoe
46-Thunderbird Lake Tahoe
48a-Wikipedia
48b-University of Nevada, Reno; Online Digital Collections
49-University of Nevada, Reno; Online Digital Collections
50-Vintage Everyday
52-Lake Tahoe Historical Society
55-Wikimedia Commons
58a-*Tahoe Daily Tribune*
58b-U.S. Federal Bureau of Investigation
60a and 60b-University of Nevada, Reno; Online Digital Collections
61a-University of Nevada, Reno; Online Digital Collections
61b-Author's Collection
62-University of Nevada, Reno; Online Digital Collections
64-University of Nevada, Reno; Online Digital Collections
65-The Western Nevada Historic Photo Collection

66a and 66b-University of Nevada, Reno; Online Digital Collections
71a-University of California, Berkley; Library Digital Collection
71b-Wikimedia Commons
72a-University of Utah; Special Collections
72b-Authors' Collection
75-Stewart Indian School Cultural Center and Museum
76a and 76b-Stewart Indian School Cultural Center and Museum
78-Wikimedia Commons
81a and 81b-University of Nevada; Reno; Online Digital Collections
84a-University of Nevada, Reno; Online Digital Collections
84b and 84c-Author's Collection
84d-newspapers.com; *Reno Gazette-Journal*
87-www.prweb.com
88-Truckee-Donner Historical Society
91-University of Nevada, Reno; Online Digital Collections
92a & 92b-University of Nevada, Reno; Online Digital Collections
95-University of Nevada, Reno; Online Digital Collections
96a-California History Room
96b-The Western Nevada Historic Photo Collection
98-*Classic Trains*
99 & 100 *Life Magazine*
101-newspapers.com, *Seattle Star*
102a & 102b-Cruising the Past
106-Welcome Collection
107a-Wikipedia
107b-Heidi Wilson Photography, with permission from North Lake Tahoe Historical Society
108a & 108b-University of Nevada, Reno; Online Digital Collections
110-University of Nevada, Reno; Online Digital Collections
111-University of Nevada, Reno; Online Digital Collections
112-University of Nevada, Reno; Online Digital Collections
113-University of Nevada, Reno; Online Digital Collections
114-The Western Nevada Historic Photo Collection
116-Wikipedia
118-*History Expeditions;* Robert Lebron
120-The Western Nevada Historic Photo Collection
122-Harvey's Lake Tahoe
123a and 123b-The Western Nevada Historic Photo Collection
124-The Western Nevada Historic Photo Collection
125-University of Nevada, Reno; Online Digital Collections
126-The Western Nevada Historic Photo Collection
128-University of Nevada, Reno; Online Digital Collections
129-University of Nevada, Reno; Online Digital Collections
130a and 130b-University of Nevada, Reno; Online Digital Collections
132-University of Nevada, Reno; Online Digital Collections
133a-The Western Nevada Historic Photo Collection
133b-University of Nevada, Reno; Online Digital Collections
134a and 134b-The Western Nevada Historic Photo Collection
136-Another Old Movie Blog
137a-www.drfreexfiles.com
137b-www.godfatherfandom.com
141-University of Nevada, Reno; Online Digital Collection
142a & 142b-University of Nevada, Reno; Online Digital Collection
144-Lake Tahoe Historical Society
148-California State Library

150